ON
COLFAX
AVENUE

ON COLFAX

AVENUE

A Victorian Childhood

Elizabeth Young

Annotation by Cade Nethercott

Colorado Historical Society
Denver

Colorado History
ISSN 1091-7438

Number 9
2004

COLORADO HISTORICAL SOCIETY

Research and Publications Office
Modupe Labode and David N. Wetzel, *directors*

Publications Director
David N. Wetzel

Colorado History **Series Editor**
Larry Borowsky

Cover Design
Mary H. Junda

The Colorado Historical Society publishes *Colorado History* to provide a flexible scholarly forum for well-written, documented manuscripts on the history of Colorado and the Rocky Mountain West. Its twofold structure is designed to accommodate article-length manuscripts in the traditional journal style and longer, book-length works which appear as monographs within the series. Monographs and special thematic issues are individually indexed; other volumes are indexed every five years. The publications of the Society generally follow the principles and conventions of the *Chicago Manual of Style,* and an author's guide is available on request. Manuscripts and letters should be addressed to: Research and Publications Office, Colorado Historical Society, 1300 Broadway, Denver CO 80203. The Society disclaims responsibility for statements of fact or opinion made by contributors.

The author's children—Frederica Bunge, Caroline Hufford-Anderson, and John David Muhlenberg—provided invaluable assistance in the preparation of this book. To them, our warmest appreciation.

—Colorado Historical Society

Detail from "Perspective Map of the City of Denver, Colo., 1889—Ellis, McDonough & Co." The author's childhood home is shown just to the right of the "Colfax Avenue" notation. Courtesy Denver Public Library, Western History Collection.

CONTENTS

Publication of this book has been made possible by a generous grant from the Volunteers of the Colorado Historical Society.

Prologue

ON COLFAX AVENUE tells the story of two childhoods: a girl's, and a city's.

The girl was Elizabeth Stoddard Young, the author of this memoir. Born in Denver on October 9, 1890, she grew up at 244 West Colfax Avenue—the present-day corner of Colfax and Cherokee, where the Denver City and County Building now stands. And that conjunction is fitting, for Denver is the metropolis whose childhood is captured herein: The city and the girl grew up together.

Though thirty-one years old when Elizabeth Young was born, Denver was still very much in its infancy, just a few baby steps removed from its frontier cradle. It possessed a full-grown urban physique—a monumental growth spurt in the 1880s had tripled its population to 106,000—yet still had a juvenile's half-formed identity. The 1890s (the years described in this book) remain among the most turbulent decade in Denver's history. The Silver Crash of 1893 blew Denver's economy to smithereens. Unemployed workers pitched their tents on the banks of the South Platte, while waves of immigrant laborers—German, Irish, Italian, Japanese—came and went in profusion. The Populists swept into power that year, then were swept out just as suddenly two years later; a vast new class of voters (women, who gained the franchise in 1893) made politics all the more unpredictable. Corruption ran rampant in Denver's police and fire departments, sparking the infamous "City Hall War" of 1894. Tens of thousands of citizens moved away during these hard times, yet Denver continued to grow, largely by annexing nearby suburbs.

It was a city still very much in the making—and Elizabeth Young's family helped make it. Her parents, Frank and Carrie Young, belonged to a small but extremely influential clique that had relocated en masse from Central City in about 1880. Denver, then a village of thirty thousand, sat on the cusp of a Golden Age—and the transplants from Central mined it for all it was worth. They founded Denver's largest banks, consolidated the city's streetcar system, ran the power company, and built the most luxurious hotels and theaters. Though less celebrated than the Tabors, Moffats, Gilpins, Cheesmans of legend, these pioneers were no less important in the city's upbringing.

Frank Young, one of Denver's leading securities brokers and investment bankers, ladled out much of the capital that fed the city's stupendous growth. More important, perhaps, he and his family taught the unschooled community some manners. "The Young home was the starting point for all Colorado cultural society," wrote the *Denver Post* in 1935, on the occasion of Carrie Young's death. "Mrs. Young formed a group which became interested in cultural functions of all kinds, tho her principal interest was in music, in which she displayed unusual talent." Of Frank Young, the *Post* eulogized: "If Denver acquired a taste for good music, as revealed thru the symphony orchestra and other delightful musical mediums, Frank C. Young was in a large degree responsible."

Elizabeth Young wrote *On Colfax Avenue* in the 1960s, toward the end of her life. Her memoir vividly captures the mix of curiosity and anticipation that animates childhood. Like any kid, she could hardly wait to find out what would happen to her next; she was dying to know "Who am I?" and "Who will I be?"

The very same might be said of Denver in the 1890s.

ON
COLFAX
AVENUE

Night Lights

When, in 1894, I had reached the age of four, I was considered old enough to dispense with the services of a nurse. The guiding star of my babyhood was Nana, my beloved Nana, who had been with us since I was born.

Nana was a plain little thing, with steel-rimmed spectacles and hair cut short like a boy's, owing to a bout with typhoid fever some years before. She always wore a neat print dress with a white apron, and since her eyesight was none too good, when we went walking, she always put on a pink sunbonnet to shield her eyes from the strong western sun. So I, too, begged for a sunbonnet, and when we started down Colfax Avenue for our daily walk—I, clinging to her hand, a smaller edition of Nana in my pink dress, white pinafore, and sunbonnet—people always turned to look at us in amusement.

Every night at bedtime she would gather me in her arms and, sitting in the little rocker before the fire, she would rock back and forth, crooning lullabies or old-fashioned Methodist hymns. When anything went wrong in my infant world, Nana was my rock and my refuge. And now I was facing the first crisis in my life. Nana was leaving me. I wept bitterly. ❧

My mother tried to comfort me. "See, we're going to move your crib right in here next to our bed," she said soothingly, as the white enameled iron crib was being pushed up beside the large, double mahogany bed in which my father and mother slept. The dismantled nursery was being done over for my sister, who was returning from boarding school to live at home in the fall. She would be going to parties and balls and would need a larger room than the one she had had heretofore, a little chamber adjoining my parents' bedroom.

"Nana is going to take care of the Tabors' little girl, Persis," my mother went on, "and she says you can come over and play with her often."

But I was not to be reconciled. I hated the Tabors' little girl, Persis, who had robbed me of Nana. As time went on, however, and I gradually became accustomed to my loss, my mother persuaded me to accept Mrs. Tabor's invitation to spend the night with Persis and Nana.

❧ For minorities and immigrants, especially women, few jobs were open in the late nineteenth century outside the domestic-service sector. Around the turn of the century, women made up 18 percent of the work force, with half employed in private homes. Child caretakers and other domestic servants typically earned room and board plus two to five dollars per week, while toiling twelve to fourteen hours per day. Laundresses took in about fifty cents daily.

2

The Tabor family has been written up extensively in the annals of the West. Old Mr. Tabor, Persis's grandfather—Horace Austin Warner, or HAW, as he was commonly known—was notorious chiefly for the great wealth he had acquired in the mines of Leadville; for the bizarre activities of his second wife, Elizabeth "Baby Doe," and their daughter, Silver Dollar; and for the Tabor Grand Opera House in Denver, on which he had spent a fortune.

I never saw old Mr. Tabor, but his son's family were friends of my parents. Mr. Maxcy Tabor, the son of old Mr. Tabor by his first wife, was the manager of the Brown Palace Hotel, one of the most famous hostelries west of the Mississippi. He was far from the blatant and boorish person that his father has always been portrayed as. He resembled his quiet Vermont mother and was an extremely handsome and prepossessing man. He had married one of the beautiful Babcock sisters, and when their little daughter, Persis, was born, it was like the advent of royalty.

Persis, too, was beautiful, but very delicate, and the city was ransacked for the proper kind of baby food to agree with her tender digestion. Since the Tabors lived in the hotel, where they occupied its finest suite of rooms, Persis was always taken for her daily outing in the grounds of the old Tabor mansion across the street. The grounds were completely surrounded by a

An infant when his parents came to Colorado in 1859, Nathaniel Maxcy Tabor grew up in Rocky Mountain mining camps and helped manage the family fortune. After his parents' infamous divorce and his father's remarriage, Maxcy remained devoted to his mother, Augusta, and stayed out of the headlines. But he kept his place among Denver's most influential citizens, managing the Brown Palace Hotel and dabbling in the mining business while helping to establish the elite Denver Club. He died in 1929—among the last of the "59ers" to pass away.

high, wrought-iron fence with a gate that was always kept locked; inside, a number of cast-iron deer disported themselves about the premises. Here Persis could be seen every day, digging alone in her sand pile, the rather pitiful figure of a wealthy child, carefully segregated from other children.☙

It was some time before my mother could persuade me to accept Nana's invitation to come and play with Persis, but eventually I went. Once the ice was broken, I enjoyed spending the night with them, particularly as I grew older. I was fascinated by the excietment and gaiety of the big hotel.

The Brown Palace was nine stories tall and built in a triangle, with the lobby open all the way up to the glassed-in roof. The elevators were not enclosed but ran in gaudy bronze cages at each corner of the building, clanging madly up and down with their occupants clearly visible from the corridors.

Standing on tiptoe or being lifted up, we could peer over the elaborate grilled railings running round the corridors and see far, far down into the lobby below, which was always bustling with activity. Bellboys laden with heavy bags rushed to and fro, escorting new arrivals to the elevators; sunburned miners, in town for the weekend, crowded up to the desk seeking rooms; mustached dandies lolled on comfortable divans and ogled the beautifully gowned women who swept through the lobby on

❧ Persis Tabor's life would follow the same boom-bust trajectory her famous grandfather's did. In 1914 she married a wealthy French businessman named Paul La Forque and accompanied him back to Paris. There she raised four children, before divorcing La Forque in the mid-1930s. In 1946, impoverished by World War II, Persis returned to Denver and worked as a wage-earning tour guide at the Windsor Hotel—which her grandfather once owned, and in which he lived after losing his fortune. In 1947 Persis moved back to France and never again visited Colorado.

their way to dinner or the upstairs ballroom, great cabbages of violets pinned to their sealskin coats, their trains held up daintily in their gloves hands. In sharp contrast, an occasional cowboy in high-heeled boots, fringed leather chaps, and a ten-gallon hat would stride magnificently through the crowd, pushing everyone out of the way.

Persis, Nana, and I always had our supper in the nurses' and children's dining room, a small anteroom near the hotel's kitchen. Sometimes the maitre d'hotel, a honey-tongued Frenchman, would come over to greet us.

"This is Mr. Frank Young's little girl, Elizabeth. She has come over to spend the night with Persis," Nana would explain.

Francis would bow graciously. "Ah, yes, I know Mr. Young. Would Mees Elizabet like a small box of candy to take home?" He would hasten out and return with a pound of Gunther's chocolates. I was entranced.

After supper, we were allowed to sit up and watch Mr. and Mrs. Tabor dressing to go out for the evening. Their suite was always bright and gay, with maple furnishings and plenty of electric lights in pink silk shades. The bedroom had a bright brass bed and a magnificent spread of white lace.

Nana would be called upon to hook Mrs. Tabor up the back, and Mr. Tabor would appear immaculate and fastidious in evening clothes. Persis' mother would kiss

The Brown Palace Hotel was brand-new during the author's childhood, having opened to great fanfare in 1892. Built at the exorbitant cost of $2 million, it was conceived by Maxcy Tabor and William Bush—the latter an ex-associate of H.A.W. Tabor and a very old friend of the author's father (see page 18). Equipped with such luxuries as steam heat and flush toilets, the Brown immediately replaced the Windsor as Denver's most luxurious hotel—an honor it has retained for more than a century.

us both goodnight, leaving a haunting scent of delicious perfume.

On Monday evenings, they were usually on their way to the opening night of the Broadway Theater across the street, which was the fashionable rendezvous for society and the goal of theatrical companies on their trips across the country. What the Broadway lacked in the gloomy elegance of the old Tabor Opera House (whose mahogany and red plush decor had caused a sensation in the 1880s), it more than made up for in coziness and charm. The Broadway was of Moorish design, and decades later would probably be seen as horribly rococo and out-of-date; but as a background for an evening when all Denver society turned out in full force, it was unsurpassed. ❀

The round boxes were set low, just above the heads of the people seated on the main floor, and extended in a semi-circle around the theatre. Everyone in the boxes, or the main floor—termed the parquet—wore evening clothes, at least on Monday nights, and during intermissions people went from box to box chatting and greeting friends.

The road companies all played Denver for a full week, but Monday night was the fashionable night. Actors loved to play the Broadway. They were not only greeted by large and enthusiastic audiences, but many of them, particularly such drawing cards as Maude Adams, Ethel Barrymore, Richard

❀ *The Broadway, like the Brown Palace, was conceived by William Bush, and seemingly for the same reason—to one-up his former boss, Horace Tabor. Opened in November 1890, the Broadway quickly supplanted the Tabor Grand Opera House as Denver's top theatrical venue. In the early 1900s the author's father acquired an ownership stake in the Broadway, which at that time was managed by Baby Doe Tabor's brother, Peter McCourt. The Broadway presented both plays and operas and continued operating into the 1940s.*

Mansfield, John Drew, and Otis Skinner, were wined and dined in private homes before or after the performance.

Two young men who served their apprenticeship in the Broadway went on from there to win fame and fortune. One, a viola player in the orchestra whose father was director of music in the Denver public schools, later headed his own band and became a supreme master of the art of jazz—Paul Whiteman. The other was an usher whose good looks, dancing feet and nimble body led him to Hollywood fame and fortune: Douglas Fairbanks.✎

Since my father was part owner in the building that housed the theater, we had the use of one of the boxes. It was not until I came east to live, many years later, that I realized what a priceless boon this was to a child growing up in the heyday of the legitimate theater. On Saturday afternoons, I was often allowed to take my friends to a matinee. This gave all of us a distinct thrill. To proceed up the long, tiled lobby and walk grandly past Joe, the smiling doorman, without showing a ticket, was something that never failed to strike awe in the hearts of my schoolmates—or to provide a momentary boost to my self-esteem, which at that time I greatly needed.

We would settle ourselves in the box, the lights would go down, and the footlights would blaze, and we would wait breathlessly for the enchanted moment when the

✎ *Paul Whiteman began his career as a bandleader at Elitch Gardens around the turn of the century. He went on to lead one of America's most successful bands in the 1920s and helped launch the careers of Tommy Dorsey and Bing Crosby. Douglas Fairbanks, Jr., one of the nation's first major movie stars, also got his start at Elitch Gardens, performing in the summer repertory theater.*

curtain would slowly rise. It might be Maude Adams sailing over the audience in *Peter Pan*, Ethel Barrymore at the height of her beauty in *Captain Jinks*, the spine-tingling suspense of Willaim Gillette in *Secret Service*, beautiful Mary Boland with Robert Edeson in *Strongheart*, or a Gilbert and Sullivan production.

When the Broadway closed for the season, we could continue to satisfy our theatrical cravings at Elitch's Gardens. This was one of the most popular theaters in the country for actors starting to play summer stock. It was on the north side of town and had been started by an enterprising citizen, John Elitch, on the grounds of the amusement park he founded. After his death, his wife, Mary, went on living there, building herself a small home in the center of the gardens. A charming, gracious woman, she cultivated a reputation across the country as the "lady of the gardens" and drew to the theater dozens of first-class actors and actresses who liked the West's hospitality and friendliness, the proximity of the mountains, and the wonderful air.

I was seldom allowed to go at night to Elitch's until I was much older, which was a great deprivation, as in the daytime it was completely devoid of glamor. The emphasis was strictly on the theater. The roller coaster and the Ferris wheel were decidedly second-rate, and the sole remaining occupants of the zoo were two mangy

The theatre at Elitch Gardens opened in 1897, presenting plays and classical music concerts every week during the summer and early fall. The summer theater company performed a wide range of plays, featuring local actors alongside rising young stars such as Edward G. Robinson and Grace Kelly. The Friday night symphony concerts, led by maestro Rafaello Cavallo, kept classical music alive in Denver for a number of years.

bears who sat on their haunches in a pit and begged for peanuts.

On May Days, the school I attended rented the big "tally ho" that was a town institution, and off it would go, bristling with children, across the city to Elitch's Gardens. This was decidedly fun. The tally ho belonged to one of the livery stables and was pulled by four horses. ❦ Since everybody wanted to sit on top, there was a mad scramble for seats, and nobody but the faculty could be persuaded to sit inside. It was so top-heavy with children clinging to the seats and hanging on by their eyeteeth that it was a wonder it didn't turn over before getting through the city.

It was after dark, however, that the Gardens reached their acme. The entire picture changed. The gardens turned into an enchanted world, with lights glowing, bands playing, and dozens of people strolling up and down munching popcorn. I was always made to go to bed promptly at 8 o'clock and would look wistfully out the window at the Rogers children next door, setting out with their parents in their four-wheeled trap for the Gardens.

My father seldom went out evenings, preferring to stay at home quietly engrossed in his reading or writing. But every now and then he would be persuaded to accompany the rest of the family to a concert or to the theater, and I would be left alone at home in our large, echoing house on

❦ *Baron von Richtofen, founder of the fashionable Montclair area in east Denver, launched the "tally ho" carriage in the 1880s to advertise his new neighborhood. The bright red, horse-drawn carriages made daily trips to downtown Denver. The Baron eventually abandoned the idea of daily excursions, but the tally-ho remained a familiar sight around town—and a particularly delightful one for children.*

Colfax Avenue. The two maids would go upstairs to their rooms in the back of the house on the third floor—miles away, it seemed to me. A tiny blob of gas would be left burning in an adjoining room, but it gave an eerie light and made flickering shadows on the ceiling that were almost more terrifying than total darkness. I would lie awake listening to the distant street noises, the whistle of the popcorn wagon on the corner, the cry of the hot tamale man as he wearily pushed his cart homeward down into the lower purlieus of the avenue. Sometimes I would hear the tramp of feet and peremptory orders in loud voices on the street outside as a newly organized fraternal group, the Woodmen of the World, practiced their marching with their pickaxes over their shoulders.

At last would come the clop-clop of horses' hooves, the soft swish of carriage wheels, gay voices, and the opening of the front door. I would draw a great breath of relief and snuggle down under the covers. The family was home at last.

The Lure of the Rockies

My father was forty-five years old when I was born. As I grew from babyhood into childhood, I knew him as a tall, slender man with a head of prematurely white hair and the face and manner of a scholar. He was not a gregarious person and, although a hospitable and charming host, cared little for crowds. He was happiest just to be in his own house, surrounded by his family. My father usually came back from his office, where he dealt in investment securities, around 4 P.M., ensconced himself in his big Boston rocker in the library, and spent the rest of the day and evening smoking innumerable Havana cigars, reading *The New York Sun,* and poring over endless papers and manuscripts. He was a New Yorker by birth and had grown up in one of the very oldest sections of the city, with the aura of its Dutch ancestry still clinging to it.

He had come to Colorado as the Civil War ended in 1865, having walked the entire distance from the Missouri River to the Rocky Mountains.❧ This feat I took in my childhood as a matter of course, since practically all the old friends of my family had come the same way, either by foot or by stagecoach (though a few arrived elegantly by private carriage hired for the journey). In their time the railroad extended no farther than Iowa. Yet my father was the last man in the world anyone would have picked out for such a formidable undertaking.

His father, Grandfather Young, was an austere and terrifying old man, looking— the only time I ever saw him, on an early occasion when I was taken east for a visit— much as the prophets of the Old Testament are portrayed, with a fiery expression and long white beard. When my father urged me to get up on his lap, I did so with reluctance, quaking inwardly. He leaned over and kissed me solemnly on the forehead. I always remembered how his beard tickled, and how I disliked it. He was a Scotch Covenanter whose ancestors had fought with the iron-willed Oliver Cromwell during the English Civil War, and his rigid pursuit of high moral purpose showed in every line of his stern and rockbound face.

The grandmother whom I never knew was said to have been a gentle and lovely woman; she had succumbed to tuberculosis at the age of thirty, leaving four children.

❧ Born in New York City on January 28, 1844, Francis Crissey Young was twenty-one years old when he came to Colorado. For a complete account of his journey west, see his self-published memoir, Across the Plains in '65 (1905).

My father had worshipped her, and when my grandfather married again, adding another batch of nine or ten children to the already crowded house, my father determined to leave home as soon as the opportunity presented itself.

The lure of the West tempted him, as it did so many other young men, and the much-heralded gold discoveries in Colorado egged him on. He would go west and seek his fortune. That he had practically no money daunted him not at all.

Nor did his lack of the physical endowments for such a journey. He was a thin, pale youth who had suffered from a severe case of typhoid fever and who had been indentured as an apprentice printer and confined to long hours in a workshop since the age of fifteen.✣

Yet when the opportunity arose to join a group of three other young men who were taking a small freighting outfit to the mountains, he accepted it eagerly, setting out with them from Atchison, Kansas, on Saturday, March 11, 1865. The West was overrun with discharged soldiers, gold-seekers, adventurers, and riffraff of all kinds. Also there was, of course, the ever-present menace of Indians. The Arapahos and Cheyennes might come swooping down at any moment out of a sandhill, shrieking war cries, and massacre the entire party. Crossing the plains could be accomplished only with the best of luck and eternal vigilance.

✣ *Young spent five years in the shop of New York printer John F. Trow. His first steady job upon arriving in Colorado was as a compositor for the* Black Hawk Journal, *operated by frontier publishing legends Ovando Hollister and Frank Hall. In his* History of Colorado *(1891), Hall wrote effusively of his former employee: "Here was such perfection of typography as no man in [Colorado] had ever been accustomed to. . . During an experience of more than twenty-five years in and about printing establishments, I have never known his equal."*

This particular little group set out on foot as soon as the sun was up, walking from sixteen to eighteen miles a day, sometimes alone, sometimes seeking the protection of a wagon train. At night they camped beneath the stars, occasionally in the teeth of a late-spring blizzard, one man always on watch beside the tethered horses.

They arrived in Denver Friday, April 21, 1865, having covered 672 miles through the thick of Indian country without losing their scalps. But on every side they saw burned stations, debris from scattered wagon trains, and skeletons of men and beast moldering on the prairie.

Before 1865, Indian attacks on travelers were rare; the "menace" the author refers to was greatly overstated. But Frank Young traveled to Colorado at a particularly dangerous time—just months after the Sand Creek Massacre. In that tragedy of November 29, 1864, seven hundred U.S. soliders attacked a peaceful Indian camp in southeastern Colorado and killed about one hundred and fifty Cheyennes and Arapahos. The following spring, the revenge-minded Cheyenne Dog Soldiers laid seige to the South Platte Trail, the main frontier highway into Denver. It became such a hazardous road that the U.S. military closed it for a time in 1865, shortly after Frank Young's journey.

After restocking in Denver, my father went directly to Central City, forty miles into the mountains. Here the rich Gregory diggings were vying with California in their stupendous output of gold. It was a bleak and barren spot. The rocky hills were honeycombed with prospect holes and yawning shafts. The scarred earth bristled with jagged stumps and scrawny underbrush. The tiny frame houses clung like limpets to the mountainside. The main thoroughfare trailed the precipitous course of the gulch, at the bottom of which ran a leaden-hued stream, murky with the off-scourings of the mines.

But in spite of the ugliness, my father loved it. It was a vigorous, exciting, carefree life, shared with thousands of other young men from all quarters of the globe.

After five or six years, when the railroad had finally succeeded in pushing its way across the continent, my mother arrived in Colorado, bringing Ella, her invalid sister, with her in the hope that she might recover from tuberculosis. For already Colorado's fame as a health resort had spread over the East. Later, when she and my father were married, they joined the little group of young people who moved to Denver and formed the nucleus of the "old" families.

Central City people were always wont to hold their heads a little higher than the residents of other mining towns.✱ Except in the first hectic days of the gold rush, Central City had always been an industrious and well-behaved community, far removed from the wild goings-on of the later bonanza camps of Leadville and Cripple Creek, and Centralites were apt to look down their noses at people from the latter localities as Johnny-Come-Latelies.

✱ *This sense of pride comes across loud and clear in* Echoes from Arcadia *(1903), Frank Young's memoir of his fifteen-year sojourn in Central City (1865-1880). Young seems to have deemed these years the most exciting of his life, and no wonder—he prospered mightily during them. In addition to succeeding professionally (as an officer at the First National Bank of Central City), Young was twice elected city treasurer and helped establish the Central City Opera (see Chapter 5).*

But by the 1880s, the heyday of the mining gold rush was over. Deep mining had taken the place of the rocker and cradle, and the romantic era of placer mining was over. The adventurers who had moved in at the first stampede had disappeared to fresher fields.

Everyone was moving to Denver, which was mushrooming all over the prairie and giving every evidence of becoming a metropolis of real proportion. Leaving the banks of Cherry Creek, where the first log and sod houses had been hastily thrown up, it was already spreading up the gentle slope later known as Capitol Hill, from whose summit the granite columns of the new statehouse came to dominate the humming city below. Horse and cable cars plied along streets whose dust had been stirred only a few years before by Concord coaches and Conestoga wagons.

A steady stream of new and eager citizens was quietly moving in and taking over.✸ The influx included shrewd Yankee merchants, professional men, lawyers and doctors, anxious to hang out their shingles in a fresh and prosperous locality; engineers, chemists, and mining specialists from all over the globe; and Englishmen and Canadians, always the first in any far-flung land, who found the open spaces and outdoor life much to their liking.

Two parallel currents co-mingled in almost equal quantities in the city's social life. One consisted of New Englanders such as my mother's family, who had been pushing steadily westward since the American Revolution, stopping along the way to build in Illinois, Iowa, and Wisconsin with a distinct Yankee flavor. The other stream, even more insistent, poured out of the South, many of whose elite families, impoverished by the Civil War, came west to make a fresh start. In the easy, friendly atmosphere of the West, these two streams mingled and fused with little postwar bitterness.

✸ *Frank Young ranked among the most prominent, and most prosperous, of the newcomers, along with a number of his old friends from Central City. The securities brokerage he co-founded, Rollins & Young (later the Rollins Investment Company), became the West's largest issuer of municipal bonds, financing school districts, transit systems, power utilities, and other public institutions throughout the region.*

16

Added to these was the influx of health seekers fleeing tuberculosis, the "great white plague," who found that the keen air and vivid sunlight were a tremendous asset in stamping out a disease that at that time was taking a terrific toll of youth.✵ "Consumption," as we called it, held no terrors for me, nor was it a subject to be spoken of in hushed and mysterious tones, as was true with adults. "So and so is out here for his health." That was all that was said.

We children took this all as a matter of course. Young men came to our house by the dozens (most of them beaux of my older sister, Eleanor), handsome young men with the telltale red flush on their cheekbones, the intermittent cough. They flocked in, fleeing the damp New England winters, the humid lowlands of Georgia and the Carolinas. Some had money and some did not. Many lived and recovered completely. Many of them entered the fine sanatoria that were springing up all over the prairies; some, without the necessary funds, spent all they had on the railroad journey and died like flies on park benches and in cheap boarding houses. Denver was drained financially to take care of all these sufferers.

Since land was to be had in abundance, houses in Denver were not scrimped for room and huddled together in pinched little blocks, as in the older eastern cities. The streets were broad and level, and each house, however modest, boasted its own yard.

✵ During the late nineteenth and early twentieth centuries, tuberculosis caused one out of nine deaths in the United States. At that time, medical science did not have a treatment, but it was widely believed that Colorado's dry air and mild temperatures could cure the sick. In reality, the climate conferred no health benefits whatsoever. But the mythical "altitude cure" for tuberculosis played a major role in Colorado's growth, bringing thousands of new residents to Denver, Colorado Springs, and other cities.

People vied with each other, by arduous irrigating, for the greenest grass. The wealthier citizens promptly erected large, handsome stone or brick mansions with generous grounds, whose iron fences often enclosed a scatttering of cast-iron stags. The acme of elegance was attained by those boasting a private ballroom, usually attached as a wing. These ballrooms, whose gilt chairs for the most part stood shrouded in linen covers, were opened periodically for a fashionable ball and in the intervening months were used for children's dancing classes, meetings of women's groups, or amateur theatricals and concerts.

Our own house was built at a time when my father's fortunes were at their high-water mark. From then on, owing to unfortunate investments and business entanglements, they began to recede, and he never again achieved the financial security that had been his when I was small. He became worried and anxious, often referring to a man named "Bush" who had gotten the better of him in some transaction. This man Bush became the evil spirit of my childhood. I pictured him as a large, fleshy man with bushy side-whiskers, always pursuing my father, who never seemed able to evade his evil manifestations. Sometimes my father would pace the floor at night with a frowning face, and, young as I was, I knew he was beset with business worries. I longed for the day when Bush would

Among his various talents, William Bush excelled at spending other people's money—but at least he spent it well. He and the author's parents met in the early 1870s at Central City, where Bush ran the best hotel in town: the Teller House. Sharing a love for music and theater, the Youngs and Bushes

come to a well-deserved end, and cease to pursue my gentle father.

My father took great pride in having made good in Colorado, in spite of the dire predictions of his more conservative family that it was a harebrained undertaking and would come to no good end. He wanted to surpass what his brothers had done, and so he did. They were satisfied to build modest homes in New Jersey and commute to New York City every day, but our house was far more modern and up-to-date.

Taken back East at the age of six or seven to visit his family, I was shocked to find that they had neither telephone nor electric lights. Our telephone had been installed when the house was built, and its large, clumsy box clung to the wall in the back entry and clanged constantly for some member of the family.

The house itself, which stood where the City and County Building was later erected, was built of red brick on a foundation of native pink sandstone in the entirely ugly style of the 1890s. But at least it escaped the brackets, turrets, and cupolas of a few years earlier. It had many advantages, too. It was large and commodious, as solidly built as the Washington Monument, and set in a fine, large yard. There were only two other houses in the block. It had a wide sandstone coping around the premises that every passing child wanted to walk on, and the big, flat horseblock in front made the best table

remained devoted friends for the next quarter-century, during which Bush became Horace Tabor's right-hand man and Denver's most celebrated hotelier. Tabor and Bush had a nasty falling-out in the mid-1880s; re-enter Frank Young, who partnered with Bush on a series of projects, including the Windsor Farm and Fairmount Cemetery (see Chapter 6). His ventures always made money, but Bush's genius lay in spending, not saving. When appendicitis claimed him in 1898, he had less than $200 in assets and more than $500,000 in unpaid debts—a fair share of which, apparently, he owed to Frank Young.

in the world for playing jacks or marbles on a fine spring day. Trees were, of course, hard to come by in this bare land, but the setting out of a number of adolescent maples and locusts, combined with the native cottonwoods, gave us all the shade we needed.

Since that was an era when interior decoration adhered to no particular pattern, people could indulge their own individual tastes. It mattered little that the great wide hall was reminiscent of an English castle, with oak-panelled walls and a beamed ceiling, and that the parlor was French, with gold-encrusted wallpaper and ivory woodwork and the heaviest of damask curtains across the enormous plate-glass window. ❧

The rooms were all large and sunny, the floors hardwood with beautiful marquetry, and the terra cotta fireplace at the end of the hall had come all the way from Italy. Since my father had indulged my mother to the extent of letting her go to Europe for the furnishings, it was indeed a house of which to be proud.

The custom that prevailed much later of leaving all the window curtains up for every passerby to see what was going on would have caused a furor at the time. Ever since Captain Rose, late of the Confederate Army, who lived around the corner, had seized an army revolver on hearing an intruder and rushed downstairs, only to be

❧ *The Youngs' house was designed by Frank Edbrooke, the architect of the Brown Palace, the Tabor Grand Opera House, and many other downtown Denver landmarks. It was probably built in 1886-87; city directories place the Young residence at 216 West Colfax from 1880 (the year the family moved to Denver) through 1886, and at 244 West Colfax from 1887 onward. However, no building permits or real estate records exist to confirm the date of construction.*

shot dead on the landing, everyone lived in mortal fear of burglars. ✻

Perhaps it was a hangover from the wild frontier days, with the ever-present dread of Indians or highwaymen, but shutting up for the night was a ritual that took time and patience—at least, it did in our house. The heavy plush portieres were pulled across the windows, and the front and back doors were fastened not only with a lock but with chains: two-inch-thick vestibule doors of solid oak swung to, closing us in as securely as if we were in a medieval fortress. The only thing lacking was a moat and drawbridge. Inside everyone locked their bedroom doors. Since hot humid nights, such as the East suffers from in summer, are unknown in Colorado, we had no need of cross-ventilation or air conditioning. With the coming of darkness, even in summer, a breeze swept down from the snow-clad peaks to the west; often under blankets, warm, secure, and comfortable, we slept.

✻ *The "captain" in question was actually Colonel Sam Rose, a well-known lawyer. On June 25, 1893, hearing what he believed to be burglars at his home at 1418 Evans Street, Colonel Rose snatched his gun and went to investigate. Halfway down the stairs the revolver "exploded," shooting Rose through the stomach. There is little doubt that the wound was accidental and self-inflicted. Whether there was actually any burglar at all remains a mystery, but the colonel's death nonetheless seems to have inspired great fear.*

New Neighbors

A year or so after Nana left us, when I was five or six, the big vacant lot next to ours was purchased by a doctor from Canada. After the large, comfortable, red brick house, about the same style as our own, had been completed and the family had moved in, I couldn't wait to strike up an acquaintance. My mother said there were five children in the family, whose name was Rogers. What joy! I pressed my nose against the window pane and watched as they ran all over the yard, yelling and skipping. Finally they all vanished inside, presumably for dinner. How I envied them! Our house was so quiet, so sedate. The rooms were always immaculate; meals were always served on time. I had no playmates at all in the neighborhood, and I kept my eyes glued constantly on the house next door. There were three girls and two boys; a noisy, happy, carefree lot.

Day after day I reconnoitered, hoping for an opening, for I would never have dared make the first step. One day when I was walking in the yard, I saw two figures on the other side of the hedge. I peered through eagerly. It was the two younger Rogers children, and they seemed to be about my own age.

Ruthie, who was a head taller than her brother, had enormous china blue eyes, and her tow-colored hair was cropped short like a boy's. Edmund, on the contrary, wore his yellow locks in long, loose curls over his shoulder, with a bang across his forehead. Since this was the era when all small boys were subjected to the craze for Little Lord Fauntleroy, the seven-year-old hero of Frances Hodgson Burnett's popular story, he also wore short knee pants and a white shirt with a wide embroidered collar. His blue eyes were as large as his sister's, and both showed distressing gaps where their front teeth should have been.

The book Little Lord Fauntleroy *was published in 1886 by Francis Hodgson Burnett and inspired a style of dressing for young boys, typically featuring ruffled blouses or laced collars underneath a jacket. The style remained popular through the late nineteenth century.*

We stared at each other curiously. What they saw was a small, thin child with straight brown hair braided in tiny pigtails and tied over each ear with a ribbon bow, wearing a plaid gingham dress and a white guimpe. We edged back and forth on each side of the fence, maneuvering for position. Finally Ruthie said, "Hello."

"Hello," I answered timorously. Would these two children want to play with me? I hoped so fervently.

23

"Come on over," said Ruthie hospitably. Carefully I ventured around the hedge into their big yard. It was a wonderful place to play, for the house sat squarely on one side of the lot, leaving the remainder in strong, thick grass with few trees or bushes to interfere with any kind of game children wanted to indulge in. ❧

❧ *The Rogerses were a distinguished bunch. The family patriarch, Dr. Edmund Rogers, was one Denver's great pioneer doctors (see next page). Eldest son James Grafton Rogers (1883-1971) served as Assistant Secretary of State during the Hoover administration and held a key intelligence post during World War II. He later served as president and chairman of the board of the Colorado Historical Society. Edmund (1891-1973) would attend Cornell and Yale, then return home to serve as one of the early superintendents of Rocky Mountain National Park.*

"Let's take off our shoes and stockings," Ruthie suggested. I stole a glance back at our house to see whether or not my mother was looking out of the window. I had never gone barefoot before; but since it was a warm day I thought she wouldn't mind. We sat down in the grass and divested ourselves of our shoes and stockings. Oh, the wonderful feel of the soft grass on one's feet. We wiggled our toes, running and shouting for joy like young colts. The hired man was cutting the grass, and we built ourselves nests of the fresh cuttings.

"Let's play cowboys and Indians," Ruthie proposed next. We found three old brooms in the Rogers' cellar, and astride them we raced back and forth around the house, screaming and yelling until the clapping of hands from our front porch was a summons from my father that I must come home to dinner. I rushed into the house, too excited to eat.

"I have some friends," I announced proudly. "Ruthie and Baby Boy. His name is Edmund, but they call him 'Baby Boy.' He has his hair done up on rags every night

24

to make it curl. She's two months older than I am and he's three years younger."

I was in seventh heaven. I had someone to play with at last. No longer did I have to entertain myself alone in the house, go downtown hanging onto my mother's hand, or tag along after my sister and her friends. The minute lunch or dinner was over, I escaped from the house and tore through a gap in the hedge to the Rogers' house. Being a big, easy-going family, one child more or less around the house made little difference. They took me in and counted me as one of their own, for which I have been eternally grateful.

Not that I was not entirely unhappy in my own house. I loved my family dearly, but they were all adults—my sister, Eleanor (sixteen years my senior), my parents, and my Aunt Hattie, each occupied with pursuits of their own. It was quite different at the lively household next door.

Dr. Rogers was a bluff, genial man, heavy set, bearded, and an almost exact counterpart of the British king, Edward VII. He was full of jokes and puns, very different from my quiet, bookish father. Sometimes on a warm summer evening, instad of taking the buggy with one roan horse in which he normally made his calls, he would get out the high-wheeled trap with his fast-stepping pair and take Mrs. Rogers and some of us children along. This was the acme of bliss. I was never allowed to go when Mrs. Rogers

Edmund James Armstrong Rogers first visited Denver in the early 1870s and relocated permanently in 1882. A physician and surgeon, Dr. Rogers attended the Royal College in Edinburgh, Scotland, and later specialized in psychotherapy. He helped establish Denver's St. Lukes Hospital.

25

or one of the older girls was going to drive. Mrs. Rogers was no mean horsewoman herself, but my mother had firm convictions that only a man could handle two horses competently.

However, if kindly Mrs. Rogers called from the front seat, "Come along, Elizabeth, tell your mother the Doctor's going to drive," I would rush home to inform the family, and Ruth, Edmund, and I would clamber joyfully up into the back seat which faced to the rear. If that was full, we three sat on the floor, dangling our legs over the side. This was the most fun. The doctor would emerge last, spring from the little seat into the driver's seat, and pick up the reins; the horses, always skittish and eager to be off, would plunge forward. We would bowl smoothly along the wide level avenues, first to Saint Luke's Hospital, where we waited while the doctor made his rounds.

In 1890 St. Luke's moved across town, from its original west Denver location to a new building at Nineteenth Avenue and Pearl Street. Dr. Rogers, one of the hospital's founders, doubtless appreciated the change of venue, as it cut his commute by more than half.

He would come back after awhile, smelling strongly of iodoform, and then perhaps we would drive far out on the prairie to the southwest in the shadow of the Rocky Mountains, where a Miss Power, a tall, spare Englishwoman and an artist, lived alone in a little cabin, fighting off tuberculosis. Sometimes Miss Power would invite us into her cabin to see her paintings. Inside, there was little room in which to move around, as the space was cluttered with clothing, paintbrushes, half-finished canvases, and odds and ends of furniture. Our hostess coughed incessantly, and I pitied her, living so far out here all by herself. But then, the view of the sun going down behind the distant ranges, which she was trying to capture on canvas, was superb, as was the evening light on the purple-shadowed plains.

Miss Power herself was charming and cordial, and she showed us a picture of her home back in England, and her rose garden, and some of the things her family had sent her. Sometimes she was too weak to be up and lay on the couch, and only the doctor went in. But as we drove off again down the rough prairie road, she was almost always standing in the doorway, gaunt and wistful, waving goodbye.

"How is she?" Mrs. Rogers would say, under her breath.

"Oh, about the same," her husband would answer evasively.

But I thought of her fits of coughing, and I felt instinctively she would never see the house in England nor the rose garden again.

School Days

The public schools of Denver were excellent, especially for such a new and relatively small city. Still, there had always been a large number of families of means who preferred to have children go to a private school, and it wasn't long before there were not only one, but two, private schools, both for girls. The boys had not fared as well as the girls. An abortive attempt had been made to start an Episcopal school for boys, known as Jarvis Hall, far out on the prairie at the eastern edge of town. But a fire destroyed the building and the effort was abandoned.

The girls' equivalent of Jarvis Hall was called Wolfe Hall. A gray stone structure on Capitol Hill, it had sort of a bastard Norman design, with many cupolas and turrets, and was surrounded by large grounds. It was supremely ugly inside and had many of the attributes of a convent. The windows were narrow, the corridors were painted a hideous dark brown, and some of the upper floors where the boarding pupils lived were cut into cubicles, like nun's cells. The four flights of stairs came down a huge echoing stairwell, where an immense bell dismally summoned students to lunch.

A great many children started their education in the kindergarten of Wolfe Hall, coming in a school bus drawn by two strapping horses. But none of us cared much for the school, and we were glad when another girls' school was started several years later.

The Wolcott School, named for the headmistress, was one of the finest schools in the West, even the country. It was not hard to get teacher material, for Denver was a healthy, flourishing city, and young women were eager to work in such attractive surroundings, so we always had the pick of the eastern women's college group.

The buildings were a great change from the gloominess of Wolfe Hall. They were of pleasant cream-colored brick of a pseudo-Spanish type, sunny and cheerful. Most of the hundred or more scholars were day pupils, but there were always a few from far-off mining towns whose parents were eager to have them take advantage of the boarding facilities.

It was more than a mile from our house, in the newer residential section on Capitol Hill. Sometimes I went alone on the trolley and sometimes, in company with several

Jarvis Hall and Wolfe Hall, two of Colorado's oldest and finest prep academies, were both founded by the Episcopal Church. The latter opened in 1867 at Seventeenth and Champa Streets, then moved in 1889 to a new building at Fourteenth Avenue and Clarkson. The boys-only Jarvis Hall opened in Golden in 1869, then burned down in 1878. But the school was not "abandoned," as the author suggests. After a decade-long dormancy, Jarvis Hall reopened in 1889, housed in a new building in the Montclair neighborhood of East Denver.

The Wolcott School opened in 1898 at the corner of Fourteenth Avenue and Marion Street.

29

of the Rogers children, I walked. Unless Edmund was with us I was the smallest, and it was hard to keep up with the hearty, athletic stride of the older Rogers girls, and it kept me going at a run most of the way. We walked to school in the morning; at midday, in the space of an hour, we walked home to lunch, which we bolted in fifteen minutes, and back to school again. Sometimes, blocks away, we would hear the buzz of the warning bell and break into a run, arriving panting and gasping as others were filing into class. I tried that for a year or two, but since we also walked home in the afternoon, my mother thought the four-mile round-trip too much for me. After that I carried my lunch in a tin box strapped to my books. I liked it better anyway, though I hated to be considered a crybaby.

There was a smattering of small boys in a ratio of one to every ten girls, and they were only allowed as far as the sixth grade. There were two boys in our class, Edgar and Ira Humphries. Edgar was a handsome boy about nine or ten, with curly black hair and brown eyes. He could run like the wind, and was always chosen first by the girls when it came to playing Prisoner's Base or Pompom Pullaway at recess.❧ Like most boys he was extremely good at arithmetic, and he was also clever at drawing. He showed us some pictures he had drawn on the bottom edges of a notebook of a cowboy riding a horse. When you flicked the

❧ *Prisoner's Base—aka "Queen of the Recess Games"—was a team-based version of "tag." It dates back at least as far as medeival France; Lewis and Clark's men played it on the trail in 1805. Pompom Pullaway, of more recent vintage, was very similar to "Red Rover."*

pages over quickly, the horse actually jumped and bucked. We were spellbound by this demonstration, never realizing that he was only employing the basic formula for moving pictures, which were to come into prominence a few years later.

I cherished a secret passion for Edgar which, alas, was not reciprocated. Instead he was much attracted by Frances M., who was an heiress and an only child whose mother indulged her to the extent of letting her wear and do anything she pleased. No wonder, I thought bitterly, that Edgar preferred her, with those beautiful clothes, to me, whose wardrobe was always chosen for strictly utilitarian purposes. In fall and winter I wore a blue serge Peter Thompson suit with a white dickey, black high-laced shoes, and black ribbed stockings. The petticoat that buttoned onto my Ferris waist was of serviceable black alpaca, with no nonsense about it. If it was very cold, I wore under this a white flannel petticoat with a scalloped ruffle, and white canton flannel underdrawers trimmed with crocheted lace.

Frances on the other hand, no matter what the weather, wore under her dark pleated skirt the flimsiest of white petticoats trimmed with rows and rows of valenciennes lace and insertion. When she ran her skirts billowed out entrancingly, showing a froth of lace. For years my idea of the height of elegance was to wear a

Almost surely Frances McClurg, the granddaughter of banking and railroad pioneer David Moffat. Miss McClurg graduated from Wolcott in 1909 (two years after Elizabeth Young) and, upon her society debut the following year, was described by the Denver Times as "the most chaperoned girl in the West"—also "the most beautiful girl in Denver," "a young genius," and "the most interesting debutante to attract the chroniclers of social happenings." The fawning article concluded: "No schoolgirl at the Wolcott school has been come in contact with the granddaughter of David Moffat without becoming her devoted friend." Elizabeth Young might beg to differ.

white lace petticoat with a dark school dress. But this I never attained.

In the same class with us also was Clara Cody, Buffalo Bill's granddaughter. She was a quiet, simple girl, quite unlike her flamboyant grandparent. We knew her only slightly, but she did take some of us to his show when it came to town, and we had the privilege afterwards of being introduced to her grandfather, shaking his hand, and gazing in awe at the splendor of his white riding suit, his white gauntlets, and his flowing white mane.🐝

To this same school, but some years behind me, also came a little girl whose name was Mamie Dowd, but she was just another day pupil, and of course nobody dreamed that she would some day live in the White House as the wife of the president of the United States, Dwight D. Eisenhower.

Miss Wolcott, the headmistress, was a typical stiff New England spinster, a finely educated woman of a prominent Connecticut family. She was a wonderful administrator but exceedingly shy and reserved; also a strict disciplinarian. I think her stiffness hid a distinct nervousness and lack of confidence, but it succeeded in holding all of her pupils at arm's length. Everybody stood in supreme awe of her, though she was the personal friend of many of our parents.

One day our sixth grade teacher was taken ill and had to leave the room in the middle of the geography lesson. I loved

🐝 *Edmund Rogers, Jr., had made Buffalo Bill's acquaintance under other circumstances: His father took him to see the "Wild West Show," and during the performance a rider was thrown from his mount and broke his leg. Dr. Rogers, with young Edmund in tow, rushed to the performers tent and found the bone protruding from the injured man's leg. Buffalo Bill himself grew pallid at the sight and deemed it too gruesome for a child. So he threw Edmund onto the back of his horse and led the boy around the ring. When Mrs. Rogers learned that Cody had comforted the boy by stroking his hair, she was aghast that such a ruffian had actually touched her son and immediately stripped Edmund down and bathed him.*

geography, and it was one of the studies I always did well in. Arithmetic was always to me a hopeless muddle, and I never succeeded in mastering fractions or square roots. I hated it from the bottom of my soul. But geography—with its colored maps and its pictures of tossing oceans, bustling cities, tropical landscapes, and strange and exotic people—I found infinitely fascinating.

When Miss Clary left the room suddenly, in the midst of a discussion about Africa, we were left to our own devices. Ira Boyd, the only other boy in the room besides Edgar, pulled a large bag of molasses candy out of his desk and obligingly passed it around to those nearest him. I selected a piece, tore of the wrapping, and thrust it in my mouth. My teeth champed down, and a gush of sickly sweet syrup filled my mouth. At that moment the door opened again, and Miss Wolcott came into the room. We all rose to attention. She cast a stern glance around the room and picked up the lesson book.

"We will now carry on the lesson where Miss Clary left off," she said briskly. She focused her eye on me. "Elizabeth, can you tell us the name of the longest river in Africa?"

Of course I knew it. Had I not read about the dark mysterious Congo, flowing through forests and jungles, the pigmies, the rain forests?❧ But I could only sit and gape at her horrified, my mouth filled to

❧ *Elizabeth was better off keeping her mouth shut: Africa's (and the world's) longest river is actually the Nile (4,241 miles), not the Congo (2,720 miles).*

33

bursting with a wad of half-chewed candy. I was completely unable to articulate. Again she asked the question. Again there was utter silence. My lips were pinched together trying to hold in the sticky mess of molasses. The others all turned and stared at me.

Miss Wolcott's face flamed scarlet. She drew herself up to her full height. "I am utterly surprised at you, Elizabeth," she said in her iciest tones. "I might have expected such rudeness from some children, but knowing your parents, I am sure you have been taught better manners. Please see me after school. Louise, what is the name of the largest river in Africa?"

I slumped into my seat, utterly crushed, amid suppressed giggles from the rest of the class. I had not only failed to answer a simple question, but I had disgraced my parents. When I went dutifully to Miss Wolcott's desk after school, hoping somehow to redeem myself, she had been called away, and I was never able to explain the situation to her afterwards. Whatever regard she had held me in because of her friendship for my family was never demonstrated again. Miss Wolcott was never close to the pupils and was rarely seen in the classrooms, and my humiliation, but I never told my parents after awhile I forgot about it.

Anna Wolcott, perhaps the finest Colorado educator of her day, launched Wolcott School in 1898, after five years (1892-1897) at the helm of Wolfe Hall. Her new institution

Coming home from school was always a series of adventures. While I was in the younger grades, and when Edmund was going to school with us, he, Ruthie, and I always walked home together, and we liked to loiter along the road. In winter we took our sleds, and if some friendly delivery wagon or coal truck was going in our direction, the driver would let us hitch our sleds on the rear of the wagon. Sometimes we would get a ride all the way home.

One wintry day we left school, pulling Edmund's big sled between the three of us. An empty coal wagon came down the street, going at a good clip. We ran after it and managed to get the rope fastened around the chain that held up the back door, regardless of the driver's yells to get off. We all piled on, and the driver looked around angrily, picked up his whip, and gave the horses a smart fillip with it. They lunged forward faster than ever, jerking the sled almost out from under us. Off we went, bouncing and bumping and threatening to turn over. Block after block sped by. The driver was enjoying himself hugely. He would teach these smart-aleck kids not to hitch a ride on his truck.

"Let go," shrieked Ruthie and I. But Edmund, who was steering, couldn't let go. The rope was stuck, and he couldn't release the sled. Willy-nilly we went, for better or worse. The coal wagon careened along, the sled behind it, swerving madly from side to side, while we clung deperately to each other and screamed at the driver to stop. He paid absolutely no attention. Down the hill we went as Broadway—a

quickly gained a national reputation for excellence, propelling Wolcott to a post on the University of Colorado's Board of Regents. She was well acquainted with the Young family; both of her older brothers—Henry R. Wolcott and U.S. Senator Edward O. Wolcott—had lived in Central City in the 1870s, when the Youngs lived there.

35

main thoroughfare—approached. We held our breath. Would we get across safely or be hit by a trolley car or another wagon? Fortunately there was little traffic, and we made it without mishap, but the pace never slackened.

On and on we went down the avenue, far past our cross street. Would the man never stop? How far from home would we be dragged? We were at least ten blocks beyond when the driver finally allowed the tired horses to come to a halt. "Gave you a good lesson, didn't I?" he shouted, as we climbed stiffly off, and Edmund managed to untangle the rope from the chain. "Guess that'll teach you kids not to hook onto wagons after this."

The wagon disappeared into the gathering dusk, and we trudged sheepishly off toward home through the snowy twilight, cold and shaken. It was a long time before we tried hitching onto wagons again.

But walking held pleasures, too. There was the drugstore located on the corner of Broadway where we often stopped to buy ten cents' worth of candy.❦ It was near the Broadway School, and we were always just ahead of the public school children, since we got out an hour earlier. There was no love lost between the Broadway children and ourselves. They considered us sissies, because we went to a private school; Edmund, in particular, was always singled out for the most cutting jibes, partly because

❦ *Most likely the Capitol Pharmacy at 1401 Broadway. For a time it was operated by pioneer druggist W.W. Beitenman, whose Larimer Street pharmacy dated to the 1870s.*

he went to a girls' school and also because he was walking home with two girls. As we were outnumbered about ten to one, we rarely retorted to these taunts, but hurried away as fast as possible.✷

The candy array was fascinating, however, and we liked to linger as long as we could to choose between red and white peppermint sticks in jars, the long strings of shoestring licorice, chewy peppermints and round sugar balls with nuts inside, and the all-day suckers, which started out as hard black balls but after determined sucking turned into one color after another, ending up in a tiny anise seed. In warm weather we usually treated ourselves to a soda—five cents for a plain one, ten with a generous helping of ice cream.

The impressive new Christian Science Church was going on up on one corner that we passed every day, and each afternoooon we were in the habit of prowling around after the workmen had left to see what progress had been made.✷ After several weeks the construction had at last reached the big dome on top. It was to be a very large church, though as yet the inside was nothing but open masonry up to the roof, with scaffolding high up under the dome. A series of ladders running up to these planks was too much of a challenge to be denied. We laid down our books.

"Let's climb up," said Edmund. It looked terrifyingly high, but none of us would

✷ *The Broadway School stood at Thirteenth Avenue and Broadway, on the site now occupied by the Colorado History Museum. In 1900, Denver School District No. 1 boasted about 12,000 students, versus about 1,500 private-school students across the city. Another 3,000 school-age children in Denver did not attend school at all— instead they worked, cared for younger siblings, or changed addresses so frequently that keeping them enrolled proved impossible.*

✷ *The Christian Science Church at Fourteenth and Logan was completed in 1901 after several years of construction. Designed by the architectural firm of Varian & Sterner, the Greek Revival edifice instantly became one of the city's most recognizable buildings. It was designated a registered Denver Landmark in 1968.*

admit to being afraid, so there was nothing to do but climb. Up and up we went, clutching the rungs and never stopping to look down. Once at the top Edmund, in the lead, started crawling on his hands and knees out on the two thin lines of scantling laid across the open scaffolding. I followed next, and lastly came Ruth. We had crawled several yards before I had the courage to peer down. There, horrifyingly far below, was the stone floor, with nothing between it and me but this narrow, frail line of boards. It was a sickening thought.

The scaffolding the Rogers children and Elizabeth Young were traversing stood five to six stories high, between the two halves of double dome—one half 47 feet high, the other 57 feet.

Out in the middle of the vast expanse of nothingness I suddenly lost my nerve. I wished with all my might we had never started this mad enterprise. But a few feet ahead of me Edmund crawled steadily along, and the way behind was blocked by Ruthie, also crawling slowly, her face set. Slowly we inched our way around the wide circle to the opposite side, where another series of ladders stood beckoning. Would we ever make it? I looked down once again and shuddered.

Suddenly we heard a man shouting at us. It was the watchman. "What in hell are you doing up there, you damned kids? Come down out of there," he shouted, stamping and gesticulating. He made so much noise I was afraid one of us would lose his precarious balance and topple over.

We crawled steadily on, the eyes of the watchman glued on our progress. Edmund had now reached the haven of the ladder and, feeling carefully for a foothold, started down. Now it was my turn. How to turn around and get my feet on the rungs without falling or tipping over the ladder and throwing us all to the floor below? I gritted my teeth and shut my eyes, gripping with all my might. The man below was holding his breath.

I swung my leg slowly and hitched my body around. Now I was safely on, at least. If I could just go down. Ruthie was above me, turning herself slowly for the descent. Edmund had reached the ground safely. I felt for each rung carefully with my foot, step after step, until I was out of danger. Solid earth at last! Never again! ❧

The watchman, white and shaken, waited until we were all three on the ground and then delivered himself of a lecture interspersed with such words as we had never heard before in our lives. Our families would hear of this. We'd get a good licking. We might have broken our necks and he'd be responsible. Quaking with fear of parental punishment as well as nervous reaction, we walked silently home. Our fears were groundless, for our parents never heard of our escapade, but it was years before I could look at a ladder without my knees beginning to tremble.

❧ *After the author's hair-raising experience, the church's builders experienced a cliff-hanger of a different sort. They planned to panel the interior entirely in white Russian oak, but supplies evaporated halfway through construction following a collapse in Russo-American trade relations. The builders pressed forward anyway and finished the interior with just one two-foot piece of the precious wood to spare.*

Opera Near and Far

Since I was the belated product of a marriage that had taken place some seventeen years before I was born, and my only sister was sixteen years older than I, it is natural that I remember my father and mother as people long past their youth. In their Central City days, they had been young and gay and lively, as I have heard since from many sources; but in my childhood they were well up in their forties and had settled down to a more or less sedate middle-aged existence.

My mother as a young woman was a high-spirited person, full of vigor and daring. She had coal black hair, complemented by bright black eyes and fine white skin. By the time she had come west some six years after my father, the railroad had succeeded in reaching Denver, and in the mountain towns life was somewhat less primitive than before. Faced with the challenge of bringing her desperately ill sister alone to Colorado in a life-saving effort that proved to have been in vain, she met the situation with courage and initiative. Neither girl had ever been to the West, nor had they any contacts in Central City. Once the long, arduous journey by train and stage was over, however, my mother placed Aunt Ella in a respectable boarding house and set out to find herself a teaching position to supplement the family income, which had been strained to the breaking point by doctors, medicine, and the expenses of the trip. She was given a position almost immediately, though she had no previous experience and no certificate other than her diploma from the Rockford Female Seminary, where she had spent two years acquiring all the education then deemed necessary for a genteel young woman. ❧

However her methods might stack up against the more diversified teaching of later years, she gave her pupils a thorough grounding in the three Rs. She insisted that they write in a legible hand, she drilled them in the fundamentals of arithmetic, and she taught them to read clearly and to spell correctly.

They didn't learn the dozens of extra-curricular items that go hand-in-hand with grade school training in a contemporary setting, but what they knew they knew well, and they had the foundation of an excellent education. One of her pupils went

❧ *Caroline Stoddard Sims was born April 21, 1846, in upstate New York and spent most of her childhood in Beloit, Wisconsin. She studied music at two conservatories back East after graduating from Rockford, then came out to Central City in her mid-twenties and taught at the Gilpin County Schoolhouse, 228 East High Street. One of the few buildings to survive the fire of 1874, the school now houses the Gilpin County Historical Society.*

from this mountainside school to attain at West Point the highest scholastic standing ever made up to that time.

My mother abhorred a poor speller. Another fetish of hers was the ability to write a good note. She judged everyone who came to our house to visit by the quality of their "bread and butter" letters, written in thanks. "Mrs. So and So is a nice, pretty woman," she would say condescendingly, "but she certainly can't write a good note."

It was, in her opinion, the hallmark of a lady as much as wearing spotless gloves and carrying a clean handkerchief. Her own handwriting was clear, firm, and beautiful, even when she had become an old lady, and many a time I have watched her laboring over a letter or a secretary's report, altering a word here, a sentence there, till it finally met her own approval. In spite of her deeply rooted convictions on certain subjects, however, she was always cheerful, gay, and fun-loving. She was full of music to her very fingertips and loved better than anything to dance. Even in her eighties she was still nimble and light on her feet. Indeed, her only vanity seemed to be her feet.

"I don't mind putting my hands into any kind of dirt," she used to say, "but I hate to step in it." She always kept her soft kid-and-leather shoes carefully polished and blackened, and the heels were straight and even.

Ours was always a musical household. Both my mother and my youngest aunt,

Carrie Young's preoccupation with letter-writing was not unusual. Victorians considered epistolography more than a matter of etiquette; they deemed it an art form, and judged the writer (especially if a woman) on everything from her mastery of language to her penmanship and her choices of stationery and ink. Those less skilled in the craft could lift eloquent notes for all occasions from letter-writing reference books such as The Pocket Letter Writer *(S.A.Howland, 1844).*

Aunt Hattie, who lived with us, were natural-born singers, with the wide mouths and full-arched, open throats so advantageous for that profession. Mother's voice was a rich, resonant contralto, while Aunt Hattie's was a clear, high soprano. It was apparent in their youth that one or the other should make some use of their God-given voices, but since my mother had been chosen to take Aunt Ella to Colorado and had settled for a husband and family in place of a profession, it was left to the youngest of the family to go abroad and study for an operatic career.

My father, too, had a great love for music, and possessed a pleasant light tenor voice. Soon after their marriage, he and my mother took a trip to Chicago, where they saw a performance of *The Bohemian Girl.* This experience filled them with such enthusiasm that when they returned to Central City, they resolved to stage their own version of *The Bohemian Girl.* ⊛

Central City had been blessed with an unusual amount of musical talent, and there were also many Welsh miners with fine voices whom they added to their number. In the transported version of *The Bohemian Girl,* my mother sang the contralto role, while my father not only carried the part of the leading tenor but acted as impresario and stage manager as well. It was his lot also, having been brash enough to make the suggestion in the first place and

⊛ The Bohemian Girl, *written by Irish composer Michael Balfe, debuted in 1843 to overwhelming success. For the next sixty years it was one of the world's most widely staged light operas, and two of its arias—"I Dreamt I Dwelled in Marble Halls" and "You'll Remember Me"—ranked among the best-known melodies of the age. The* Bohemian Girl *remained the most popular English-language musical until the rise of Gilbert and Sullivan in the 1880s.*

43

feeling responsibility for the performance, to hire the hall, engage the orchestra, write the press notices, print the tickets, and auction off the seats.

Costumes and scenery had perforce to be created by the company itself in the absence of any commercial stock, but they set to work with the skill and ingenuity which characterized all early western settlements thrown on their own resources.

A few snags developed. For example, one gentleman in the chorus was the proud possessor of a Highland tartan. Fancying himself in this garment, he insisted upon wearing it, regardless of the fact that the story was set in Bohemia.

Uniforms for an Austrian patrol were rather difficult to come by, since no uniforms of any kind had been seen in Central City since the Sand Creek Massacre, when 1,200 U.S. troops launched a surprise attack on a surrendered and partially disarmed Cheyenne Indian camp in south-central Colorado in November 1864. Eventually, however, a handful of Union Army veterans were rounded up, and the uniforms they lent passed muster with an audience not too familiar with Austrian liveries.

There was no lack of stringed instruments for the orchestra, but the only cornet in town was owned by an old German man. He dearly loved to tootle but was so deaf from his daily occupation of hammering boiler iron that he had to be provided with

The performances took place April 18-19, 1877, at the cramped Belvedere Theatre, Central City's only entertainment hall after the 1874 demise (by fire) of the Montana Theater. It marked the Colorado debut of the author's musically gifted aunt, Hattie Louise Sims (see pages 45-49), then just fifteen years old. The ubiquitous William Bush (see page 18), manager of the Teller House, also had a prominent singing role. For Frank Young's detailed, and highly amusing, recollections of the production, see Echoes From Arcadia *(1903).*

44

special cues to prevent him from issuing a blast at the wrong moment.

In spite of these minor discrepancies, the performance was a huge success.✻ In all the mountain towns the talk had been of nothing else for weeks before, and two performances were hardly enough to accommodate the crowds that piled in from the surrounding countryside as well as from Denver, which sent a large contingent. This production was to make history, not only its own right but also because it paved the way for further amateur performances and, according to a friend of my father, gave birth to the idea that Central City should have its own opera house.✻ This institution, funded by civic-minded inhabitants (of whom my father was one), was subsequently erected in 1878.

In the next century, when Central City underwent a major restoration and became a popular tourist destination, the Opera House reopened and attraced audiences from across the country.

Aunt Hattie had come to live with us after a tragic illness had ended all her hopes of an operatic career. Many years my mother's junior, she possessed an oustanding voice, even at seventeen years of age. Her instructor back in Wisconsin, where the family lived, insisted that she cultivate this talent. My grandparents, scraping together what they could from their remaining resources (sadly depleted

✻ The Rocky Mountain News *raved: "Unquestionably this performance was at once the most ambitious and the most successful ever given in the state." After two sellout engagements at the Belvedere, a theatrical promoter tried, without success, to engage Young and his troupe for a run of Denver shows.*

✻ *Actually, the idea of an opera house for Central City had been hatched long before. However,* The Bohemian Girl *played a crucial role in bringing the dream to fruition, because it demonstrated that such a venue could draw big enough crowds to support itself financially. The production also generated a small profit, which Young donated to the nascent opera-house fund.*

since Aunt Ella's illness and death), finally agreed to send her to New York City for further education.

For a green little girl from the West, going to that great city alone was an adventure fraught with pitfalls and hazards, all of which was constantly impressed upon her by various members of the family.

Nevertheless she set off, and soon was duly established in a discreet boardinghouse under the chaperonage of friends of my grandmother, who looked carefully after her comings and goings. There she studied with one of the finest voice teachers in the country, and before long, at the age of eighteen, she was soloist in Dr. Henry Ward Beecher's Plymouth Church in Brooklyn and was being engaged for concert work.

Born in 1862, Hattie was fifteen years younger than the author's mother. While still in her teens, she sang with the New York Symphony Orchestra, the Boston Symphony Orchestra, the New York Oratorio Society, and the Handel and Haydn Society. The Boston Herald lauded her "facile execution" and "high artistic style," while the New York Tribune hailed Hattie as "one of the most talented and popular young vocalists" in America.

That, insisted my grandmother, with her staid New England background, was as far as it was necessary for her daughter to go. All she had wanted was for little Hat to learn to become a voice teacher and to sing in church choirs. But her teachers thought such a voice wasted on choir singing: She belonged in opera. So when her mother's reluctant consent was finally obtained and the necessary funds raised, off she went to Italy to study under the great Italian maestro Giovanni Battista Lamperti.

There was little glamor at that time in learning the essentials of an operatic career. It took years of study and application, day after day of hard, grinding work, learning languages, singing scales, acquiring the fundamentals of stage business. Along with this, Aunt Hattie memorized all the roles that were a must for an operatic diva, knowing them backwards and forwards, so if a star was taken suddenly ill, she could step into her shoes at a moment's notice.

Lamperti was a difficult taskmaster. He screamed at Hattie, he waved his arms, he stamped on the floor and made contemptuous noises. He forced her to work, work, work. Once in a while, when she was on the verge of giving it all up and coming home by the next steamer, he would toss her a word of encouragement. At last he considered her fit to sing in some of the smaller Italian opera houses.

Lamperti (1839-1910), the son of the famous voice teacher Francesco Lamperti (1813-1892), taught many of the era's greatest singers, including Irene Abendroth, William Earl Brown, Roberto Stagno, and Herbert Witherspoon. His Techniques of Bel Canto (1905) became a standard teaching text.

Her first appearance created a furor. The volatile Italians loved the fresh, sparkling young voice, the lovely smile which was her greatest charm, the ease with which she sang their own language. They adored her. They sent her great baskets of flowers. They laid their hearts at her feet. But, decreed the maestro, she was a long way yet from being ready for the big cities. He would let no one get out of his studio who was not a finished product. But she was conscientious, realizing the amount of money being poured out for her expensive education.

My father, abroad on a business trip, went to Italy to hear her and wrote back to my mother that her voice was superb; he had no idea little Hattie would develop into anything so magnificent. In another year or so she would be ready to come back to America in triumph.

But, alas, she had everything to make her a complete success except one traint: physical stamina. High-strung and sensitive, she could not cope with the demands of the hard, grinding life. She was alone in a strange country, desperately homesick, and she also lacked the drive and determination that are the hallmark of the successful artist. Coupled with the strain of a broken engagement, she collapsed. The kindly London physician who counseled her said, "You have the voice, the personality, the intelligence, but you haven't the self-assurance or the physical hardihood for a professional career. Go back home, marry a nice man, and raise a family."

My grandmother wrote, "Come home. You are ill, discouraged. The life is too hard. I never held with a stage career anyway."

It was a heartbreaking decision, but a prolonged nervous breakdown settled the question. The career begun so brilliantly had come to an end. And so she came back to this country to take up her life again. No one ever heard her utter a word of complaint. Living with us, she started a studio not far from our house, ❦ where she taught a generation of younger singers the fundamentals of the old Italian bel canto. She also became the director of one of the finest women's choruses in the West. She

❦ *Hattie's studio stood at 1518 Lincoln Street. Her many prominent students included Florence Lamont Hinman, founder of the University of Denver's Lamont School of Music.*

was from that time on a leader in the city's musical life.

I loved her devotedly. Having never married, she looked on me as her own child, and I was closer to her in many ways than to my mother, who was so much older and so much more of a disciplinarian. All children loved Hattie, for she had a vivacious charm, a sense of humor, and a sweetness that appealed to persons of all ages. Although she was no churchgoer, and as far as I know had no formal religion, she was herself the embodiment of optimism, courage, and unselfishness.

Undaunted by the disappointment that would have withered a lesser soul, she picked up the threads of her life and carried on, with never a backward look at the career she had given up. She never sang again in public. Only now and then in her lessons would she occasionally demonstrate how a phrase should be sung, and for a minute the studio would resound to the clear, brilliant voice—briefly only, but long enough to give evidence of its former greatness.

I saw very little of my sister, Eleanor, during these early years. She and I moved in two different worlds. When I had eaten breakfast and was ready to start for school in the morning, her door would usually be closed and the household hushed.

Ellie was still asleep, having come in late the night before. After completing her schooling in the East, she had come home

Hattie spent eighteen years (1896-1914) as director of the Tuesday Musical Club, the largest amateur orchestra in Denver. The organization staged from three to six concerts a year and sponsored special engagements by visiting artists of national and even international renown. Hattie maintained rigorous admission standards, basing membership on actual musical ability rather than mere social standing. Even so, various intimates of the Young family (including Maxcy Tabor's wife, Laura) belonged to the club, as did both the author and her sister.

to be launched into society at a "coming-out" tea, where she was formally introduced to all my mother's friends and their daughters, most of whom she had known since infancy. She was now considered eligible for matrimony.

But matrimony, for some reason didn't develop—chiefly, I suppose, since she had so many beaux to choose from she could never make up her mind which one to take. At that time the city was flooded with dozens of eligible bachelors from the East, some out for their health, some to make their fortune, and some just to have a good time.

❦ Born at Central City in 1874, Eleanor Young was an oustanding violinist and a featured performer in Aunt Hattie's Tuesday Musical Club. She also belonged to an exclusive Denver social set known as the "Sacred Thirty-Six," founded by Louise Crawford Hill, a daughter-in-law of Nathaniel Hill (one of the Young family's many old Central City friends). Eleanor chaired the Denver chapter of the Red Cross during World War I, and she also held membership in the Society of Colonial Dames. Never married, she died in Virginia in 1941.

When I was undressing and going to bed at night, I would sometimes run in and perch on the bed to watch her getting ready for a party. Unlike my mother and aunt, whose coiffeur was their greatest problem—and who spent hours toiling with curling irons, rats, and switches before they achieved a satisfactory hairdo—my sister had hair that curled naturally and grew beautifully around her face and the back of her neck. All she had to do was to run a comb through it, make a little knot on the top of her head, and thrust in a few pins. As she stood radiant in a ball gown, I often wondered if, when I grew up, I would be half so beautiful or so popular. The telephone rang incessantly for Eleanor with inviations to dinner, to the theater, or perhaps only "to call."

This last meant that some self-conscious young gentleman, usually a newcomer to town, arrived about 8 P.M. and was ushered into the parlor, where he sat stiffly on a gilt chair until my sister came downstairs. Then they both sat there conversing nervously in full hearing distance of my father, who sat in the library reading and indicating by loud coughs or rattling his newspaper when he considered it time for the caller to take his leave. At 11 o'clock he never failed to stride across the hall to the dining room, make up a pitcher of ice water, and carry it ostentatiously upstairs. This final gesture usually had its effect.

"Dating" at that time was fraught with difficulties, since there were no movies to retreat to and no automobiles to go riding in. Unless the suitor had a horse and vehicle of his own, he either had to hire one from the livery stable or be content with the trolley car. A few intrepid souls had horseback parties, but this was usually limited to house parties in the mountains.

The coming of the bicycle, though, helped a good deal. ⁑ My sister, who quickly learned to ride one, donned her divided skirt, a stiff mannish shirt, and a sailor hat and set off on Saturday afternoons on a tandem with her beau to the races at Overland Park. The street in front of our house, being wide and level and not too much travelled, was a great place to practice bicycling, and one of our amusements on summer evenings was to watch the first attempt of some rider, generally a woman,

⁑ Recreational bicycling boomed all over the world in the 1890s, and Denver was no exception—by mid-decade the city had thirty-five retailers and fifty-five repair shops. Women in particular embraced the new pastime, as it freed them from the corset and increased their mobility considerably. Susan B. Anthony said: "The bicycle has done more for the emancipation of women than anything else in the world."

as she careened back and forth across the street while the instructor ran alongside shouting encouragement.

Often on Saturday afternoons one young man or another would drive up to our house in a bright runabout or a high dog cart, and my sister would go off with him to drive.❧ On rare occasions, the town's big "tally ho" would draw up to the house bustling with men and girls off for an afternoon's outing, their excited voices carrying across the lawn. Very occasionally some young scion would rent it, complete with liveried men who sat on the box and a red-coated bugler in the rear, and take a group to the races at Overland Park.

Being a person of varied talents, my sister was always the first to take up the latest fad to strike the public fancy, and her room was usually cluttered with the implements of whatever that might be. There was the china painting craze, and then the sketching and coloring craze, when her table was littered with boxes of half-dried paint and tumblers with brushes soaking in them. These were cast aside for the wood- and leather-burning period, when the house smelled like burnt steak and Indian heads appeared on cigarette boxes, sofa cushions, or merely wooden plaques. After this we suffered through the hammered-brass era, when the house resounded to the pounding of nails into sheets of brass for candlesticks, lampshades, and other "objet d'art."

❧ *The dog cart and runabout were both two-wheeled, one-horse carriages—the type of cheap, sporty transportation that might appeal to a bachelor and/or his date. The dog cart, conceived for hunting parties, was so named because it originally provided extra floor space for bloodhounds. The runabout's chief assets seem to have been affordability and ease of maintenance; it was the Victorian era's answer to the Volkswagen Beetle.*

In later years, her efforts turned from temporary hobbies to a more enduring pursuit. As a violinist, she was a skilled and accomplished amateur, having studied in Paris for three years. Her knowledge of violins in time came to be expert.🕸 She spent hours haunting second-hand shops, talking with Italians, Poles, and Russians about the merits of some old fiddle she had found hanging on the wall. She would bear it home in triumph, feeling she had made a bargain, and always hoping it might be the work of some old master. Donning her work clothes, she would proceed to take the varnish remover and sandpaper and scrape it down to the bare wood. If it didn't turn out to be an undiscovered Stradivarius, Amati, or Guarnerius, it was at least, after she had refinished it, a far better instrument than when she had bought it. In the end she had a very creditable collection.

🕸 *In the early 1900s, Eleanor and two friends bankrolled the Ferenczy-Rushcenberg Violin Company, headed by world-famous violin maker Karoly Tomasowzkyj de Ferenczy. The venture earned Eleanor considerable notoriety but, alas, few profits; when Ferenczy (best known as creator of the "Cremonese varnish") died in 1908, the company folded.*

ON COLFAX AVENUE: A PHOTO ALBUM

Photographs courtesy of
Frederica Bunge, Caroline
Hufford-Anderson, and John
David Muhlenberg

This page: Four faces of childhood—Elizabeth Young in the 1890s.
Facing page: Top: Elizabeth Young flanked by Ruth and Edmund Rogers. Bottom: The Young abode at 244 West Colfax Avenue.

This page: Top left: Eleanor Young at about age ten (roughly 1885).
Top right: Frank Young. Bottom: Eleanor Young (left) and Hattie
Louise Sims (right) in the family music room.
Facing page: Two interior views of the Young home.

Facing page: Top: Carrie Sims Young seated in the Young home.
Bottom: The Young family dining room.
This page: Elizabeth Young Muhlenberg in the 1960s.

Sundays

Sundays were, in our house, quite set apart from the rest of the week. On Sundays the whole city was as sedate as a New England village, chiefly, I suppose, because there was little opportunity for its being anything else. Even the Curtis Street Theater, home of lurid melodramas such as *Nellie, the Beautiful Cloak Model* and *Bertha, the Sewing Machine Girl,* closed its doors.

This was before the era of country clubs and automobiles. Between the poor condition of the prairie roads and the absence of any place to go save Colorado Springs, seventy miles away, most of the population stayed within the city limits. People generally went to church in the morning, had a heavy Sunday dinner at midday, and spent the rest of the day sleeping, walking, riding about in carriages, or paying calls.

In our house there was a tacit code of observance of the day. My father, and in general my mother, went to church in the morning, and I was expected to go to Sunday school. We went through the same ritual for Sunday dinner every week: roast beef, Yorkshire pudding, mashed potatoes and peas in the summer, turkey in the winter, and of course, ice cream. I never went to see the Rogers children on Sunday, nor was I allowed to go out for any kind of boisterous play. Aunt Hattie usually spent the day at home, since she worked hard during the week; on Sunday mornings she slept in, then attended to personal chores.

One spring, on a bright Sunday morning, my father announced that instead of going to church as usual, he was going out to the Windsor Farm to look things over, and would anyone like to come along? ❀

Since going to the big dairy farm where we got our milk (and in which my father had an interest) involved a ride of five or six miles on the cable cars, this invitation was addressed primarily to me, for he knew I was aching to go. My mother, Aunt Hattie, and Eleanor all declined, but I accepted with alacrity and ran to get ready.

The invitation put me in high feather. I had not only avoided the obligation to go to Sunday school, but as it was early May, I had just been allowed to discard my heavy underwear. This rid me at last of the bulky indignity of my long underdrawers, which always made such an unsightly lump at the top of my shoes.

❀ *The ever-present William Bush (see page 18) established Windsor Farm in 1885 to supply his Windsor Hotel with milk, eggs, and cheese. Frank Young bought a stake in the farm in 1890 and purchased it outright in 1894, leasing the land to a couple of very capable farmers named Mike Penrose and Brown Cannon. Under their supervision, Windsor Farm became Denver's premier dairy supplier, with a large creamery downtown on Blake Street and more than a hundred delivery routes throughout the city. The farm remained under Young family ownership until 1927.*

Moreover, my mother said I might wear the new lilac-sprigged dimity dress which Mrs. Tracy, the seamstress, had just finished. I loved the clean, sweet smell of it as I slipped it over my head. I found my Leghorn hat with its wreath of daisies, snapped the elastic under my chin, and announced that I was ready.

My father was waiting in the hall. He put on his derby hat and picked up the cane he always carried, and we set off for the car line, two blocks away. I skipped along beside him holding his hand. My legs in their thin lisle stockings and low brown shoes felt immeasurably light and free.

"Please, Papa, let's sit in the little outside seats," I begged as the car came in sight. Accordingly we perched ourselves in one of the back seats, right over the wheels. It faced sideways, bounced up and down with the motion of the car, and gave one a pleasurable thrill as we skimmed along, the wind whistling in our faces.

We rode up the gentle slope of Capitol Hill through the newer residential districts. When we reached the far outskirts of the city, the neat brick houses petered out into sod and adobe houses, tar-paper shacks, and straggling chicken ranches. Here we changed to a horse car, a small yellow vehicle with two parallel rows of seats upholstered in carpeting. It was drawn by a sturdy white horse, which plodded along sedately while the driver chewed tobacco,

Elizabeth and her father must have picked up the Colfax Electric Railway at its western terminus (the intersection of Colfax and Broadway) and ridden the entire length of the line to its eastern terminus at

56

spat copiously out the window, and idly slashed with his whip at the huge yellow sunflowers growing along the track. At the end of the line, far out on the eastern prairie, the car came to a stop and deposited us in the dusty road to await the farm wagon.

We stood still and looked about us, two lonely figures in all this emptiness. On three sides, the vast brown plains swept away to the sky line; but across the entire western horizon stretched the mighty barrier of the snowcapped Rockies, towering into the infinite blue. ⊛

The bobbing car on which we had been riding was disappearing down the single track toward the city. The sun shone down hotly. The only sound was the ecstatic carol of a rising meadow lark. The air was clear and bracing. I drew in great breaths of it. If only I had a horse and could gallop over those miles and miles of far-reaching plains, unbroken by a single house, fence, or piece of vegetation.

I glanced up at my father. He was standing quietly, his hands on his cane, his eyes far away on the glittering summit of Longs Peak. I knew that he loved the mountains and the rolling plains just as I did.

Before long, the farm wagon came jolting along the dry, sandy road. I scarcely recognized the driver, Mr. Anderson. Every morning he came down the alley to our back door in his little one-horse milk wagon, carrying a huge can.

Yosemite Street, three and a half miles distant. After transferring to the horse car, they would have ridden south another mile and a half to the farm.

⊛ *The farm lay just east of Fairmount Cemetery (see page 59) and south of the future Lowry Air Force Base, near the present-day intersection of Alameda and Dayton. The bare prairies described here would remain undeveloped until after World War II, when Denver's sprawl finally overtook the site. The dairy farm closed in the 1950s, and in 1962 the old milk-cow pastures gave rise to Windsor Gardens, one of the first condominium developments in the United States.*

Wearing work clothes, he would stride into our kitchen pantry and pour out quarts of milk into the flat pans set out for the purpose. Sometimes Binnie, the cook, would let me take a spoon and skim off the leathery cream for our morning cereal.

But today Mr. Anderson had on his black Sunday suit, and his sunburned face looked redder than ever against his stiff white collar. We climbed into the buckboard and, while my father and Mr. Anderson discussed farm matters and argued the relative merits of William Jennings Bryan and William McKinley in the upcoming presidential election, I looked at the sand hills bordering the road on either side. They were alive with little lizards and horn toads, which made delightful pets when kept in a shoebox and fed on flies. They loved to have their backs scratched and would dart out their tongues with pleasure. There were also innumerable prairie dog settlements, whose inhabitants sat up and regarded us inquisitively out of their black, beady eyes.

When my father had finished his business at the farm and we had inspected the rows of gentle Jersey cows, with their brown eyes and velvety flanks, the obliging Mr. Anderson brought out the wagon again and drove us the three miles to Fairmount Cemetery, where my maternal grandparents were buried. This was our largest and newest cemetery and had been started recently by a group of men, includ-

The Bryan-McKinley discussion could have taken place in either 1896 or 1900: Both elections pitted Democratic nominee Bryan against the Republicans' McKinley, with McKinley winning both times. Bryan also ran in 1908, against William Howard Taft, and lost again. Yet he carried Colorado in all three elections, polling an incredible 84 percent here in 1896. Frank Young, a pious Republican, no doubt voted against Bryan all three times.

ing my father, to take the place of the old Riverside burying ground along the banks of Platte Creek, which held the bones of the earliest prospectors and settlers. ❧

It was not at all like cemeteries in the East that I had seen, where weeping willows and quantities of shade trees and bushes sheltered the monuments. Rather, it was primitive and bare, with hardly a tree in sight except for those imported at great expense and set out over some loved one's grave. Still, the lawns were green and well kept, and the view of the mountains more than compensated for the lack of shrubbery. Moreover, said my father, now that they had begun irrigating, it would soon be as verdant as any spot in the East.

We walked over and stood on our own plot, looking down at the simple white headstones. Here my mother's parents lay side by side, along with Aunt Ella, whose trip to Colorado with my mother had come too late; her tuberculosis had advanced too far to allow her to respond to the dry air and sunshine, and she had died while still a young woman.

My grandparents, like many New Englanders, had migrated west in stages, from Connecticut through upper New York state to Wisconsin. Eventually, yielding to my mother's pleas, they had travelled in their old age from Wisconsin to Colorado. It was a long way from home to be buried, I thought, standing in front of their graves.

❧ *Opened in November 1890, Fairmount Cemetery was yet another collaboration between Frank Young and William Bush. Both men sat on the original board of directors, with Young serving a two-year term as president. In 1893, Bush and Young built a three-mile streetcar extension, the Fairmount Railway, linking the cemetery to the main line's eastern terminus at Quebec and Eighth Avenue. The new transit route made Fairmount extremely popular among Sunday day-trippers, who enjoyed the expansive views and finely manicured lawns.*

Still, this was a pleasant place to lie, with the sun pouring down out of the blue sky and meadowlarks and the mountains standing guard forever.

Were we to stay at home on a Sunday afternoon, we could expect to hear the doorbell ring often, for dropping in or coming to call was a major social activity. My mother was "at home" to ladies of her acquaintance one weekday afternoon, and told the world so by a little note engraved on her visiting card.

"Every other Tuesday," it said. Then we would expect white-gloved ladies to drive up ceremoniously to the horse block in their Victorias or broughams, drop their cards on the silver salver in the hall, and proceed to the parlor, where my mother waited formally to receive them. Fifteen minutes was the general length of time for a formal call. Occasionally my mother and sister would pick a nice day, hire a carriage (since we had none of our own), and proceed to pay off all their calls. If it was a particularly pleasant day, they might count on getting in as many as fifteen calls in the afternoon, as half the people could be counted on to be out.

On Sundays, it could be expected that many married friends and single people would drop in at our house, especially since its central locations made it ideally suited to this custom. Mr. and Mrs. Thatcher were

Both the Victoria and the brougham were lightweight, one-horse carriages. The open-roofed Victoria was a "see-and-be-seen" vehicle, perfect for shopping outings and social calls. The hard-topped brougham, popular at mid-century among wealthy Britons, was redesigned (and repriced) in late nineteenth-century America as a luxury town car for the upper-middle-class urbanite.

usually the first to arrive in their Victoria, Mrs. Thatcher, a small plump woman in black satin and jet, carrying a little black silk sunshade. They were my parents' oldest friends, having known each other since Central City days. Reversing the usual procedure of young couples intending to settle in Colorado, they had been married in Central City and had made their wedding trip east instead of west, undertaking what was then the dangerous trek back across the plains to the bride's old home in Missouri. Indians lay in wait, and the travelers sat for seven days and nights in the cramped confines of the stagecoach, Mr. Thatcher with a loaded rifle always across his knees, ready to shoot his bride and himself should they be unable to ward off an attack. Fortunately the trip was made without any untoward incident other than the ordinary discomforts of the road.

Mr. Thatcher was an affable and courtly Kentuckian with a florid complexion, a mane of snowy hair, a white goatee, and twinkling blue eyes. He could have passed anywhere for the Kentucky colonel depicted on an advertisement for bourbon. Though my parents had known them intimately for over twenty-five years, and the men were Frank and Joe between themselves, I never heard the ladies address each other in any way but as Mrs. Young and Mrs. Thatcher. We occasionally referred to "Uncle Joe" within the family, but we

Frank Young learned the finer points of his profession from Joseph Addison Thatcher, one of Colorado's first and most influential bankers. The mentorship began in 1866 at the Central City bank of Warren Hussey & Co., where Thatcher (then general manager) hired Young as a bookkeeper. Thatcher bought the bank in 1870 and reorganized it as the First National Bank of Central City in 1874, increasing Young's responsibilities at each step. (Young repaid the favor by saving the firm's records and currency from a devastating fire in 1874.) In 1884 Thatcher established the Denver National Bank and headed it up for the next thirty-plus years. His importance was such that on the day he died (October 25, 1918), every bank in Denver closed.

never called him that to his face, though he never failed to greet each one of the women, except my mother, with a hearty smack. But we would never have dreamed of calling Mrs. Thatcher "Aunt Fannie."

Perhaps it was her position as wife of the president of one of the largest banks, or perhaps her upbringing on a southern plantation, where she had been accustomed to the deference of servants, but she always stood very much on her dignity, demanding and receiving a great deal of homage. Mrs. Thatcher was unsurpassed in every phase of the housewifely arts. Her house was the most perfectly run, her lace collars were the whitest and the finest, her recipes and her knowledge of cookery unrivalled. Everything that Mrs. Thatcher attempted must result in as near perfection as possible. The Thatchers even did their washing on Saturdays instead of Mondays, thereby getting ahead of the world by one day.

She may have been fussy, but Frances Kirtley Thatcher was one of Denver's most generous philanthropists. Over the years she raised tens of thousands for St. Luke's Hospital, the Young Women's Christian Association, St. John's Episcopal Church, and many other local institutions. She also helped establish one of Denver's first kindergartens, providing a model later adopted by the public school system.

Needless to say, they had no children. I often wondered, when we were invited to an occasional Sunday dinner, how a child would have fared in that immaculate house, where we sat stiffly on the edges of the satin chairs, conversing politely. No small feet would have been permitted to mar the brilliant polish of the floors, nor childish hands to touch the expensive pieces of bric-a-brac standing at attention on the tables. My father, having been best man at their wedding, never failed to send Mrs.

Thatcher a dozen red roses every year on the anniversary of the occasion, receiving within twenty-four hours an acknowledgment on the heaviest white note paper, beautifully expressed and exquisitely penned. In spite of the overtones of formality that tinged their relations, their friendship was a warm and deep one, which lasted close to half a century.

The Thatchers usually arrived punctiliously around 3 o'clock in the afternoon and seldom lingered. They stayed about half an hour, when their place was taken by Colonel and Mrs. Randolph. They were also old Central City people and had come originally from Virginia, where Mrs. Randolph had been one of the outstanding beauties of her day.

They had come west on their wedding trip but had not been as fortunate as the Thatchers in their experience. They left Atchinson, Kansas, in a stage with seven men and two women. It was a beautiful August morning in 1864, and the journey was for some time without incident, though they had been warned of Indian atrocities and the stagecoach station at Liberty Farm had just been burned. Leaving the Big Sandy River, the stage crested a hill and entered a narrow spur bordered on each side by a deep ravine, known as the Narrows. Just as the coach was about to begin the descent to the bottomlands, the driver saw about thirty yards ahead a band

Col. George E. Randolph was a bona fide war hero, having fought with distinction in the Civil War at Gettysburg and Bull Run. A successful owner and broker of mine properties, he served in the Territorial Legislature and as mayor of Central City, then moved to Denver in 1883 and took over the Denver City Railway Company. Within six years Randolph had transformed the horse-car network into an all-electric cable-car system, one of the world's first. He later headed up Denver's public works department under Mayor Robert Speer.

of fifty or more Indians. Wheeling his horses in the narrow road, an almost impossible feat, he ordered the passengers to hold on and keep their seats, then began a desperate retreat over the road they had come.

The Indians immediately gave chase, the coach rocked and swayed, threatening momentarily to overturn. The driver, a coolheaded young man named Emery, lashed the terrified horses into a dead gallop and managed to keep ahead of their pursuers, though an arrow grazed his shoulder and another cut the rosette off the head of the wheel horse.

Ahead were two abrupt turns in the road where the coach would have overturned had Emery not brought it to a complete halt. This he proceeded to do, to the intense dismay of the passengers. But Emery knew what he was doing. About a mile ahead was an ox train, and the drivers, sensing the situation, frantically corralled their wagons. The careening coach with its exhausted horses galloped into this shelter. ❧

The Indians, daunted by this defense, gave up the chase and circled away in the distance. The shaken passengers climbed down, embraced the driver, complimented him on his courage and good judgment, and eventually made their way to Denver in safety. Later they presented him with a gold ring with their names inscribed in it, in memory of his level-headedness in saving the lives of nine people.

❧ *The Narrows escape occurred on August 9, 1864, on the Overland Trail in the vicinity of present-day Hastings, Nebraska. The stagecoach driver, Robert Emery, was the brother of road agent Charles Emery, who operated the Liberty Farm station and had survived the attack there. Two days after the Narrows incident, Territorial Governor John Evans issued an edict*

Mrs. Randolph, though long past her youth when they came to our house, was still an outstanding beauty with great dark eyes, grey hair swept back from a marvelous brow and a magnificent carriage. It was she who had been chosen to lead the grand march with the Grand Duke Alexis of Russia when he came west on his famous buffalo hunting trips in the 1870s.

Among visitors to our house, bachelors were often the first to arrive. Gentlemen who knew Aunt Hattie thought Sunday a good day for calling, since she was busy the rest of the week. My father, after a glance out the window, would go to the foot of the stairs and call in a stage whisper, "Hattie, I see old Besley coming across the street."

Groans from upstairs. "Tell him I'm out or away or something. I'm busy. I won't waste time on that old nincompoop any more," she would reply. And upstairs she would stay, quietly attending to her own pursuits, while my mother and father patiently entertained old Besley, who was a bore of the first water.

Following on his heels would come Mr. Von Shulz. This quite distinguished-looking gentleman, who bore the title of baron in his native Germany but had droppped it over here, could often be seen strolling on pleasant days along the broad avenue of Capitol Hill, accompanied by a huge St. Bernard dog. He would park the dog on our front porch, where the animal lay quietly

authorizing Coloradans to "kill and destroy . . . hostile Indians." And two days further on, he formed the infamous Colorado Third Volunteers—perpetrators of the Sand Creek Massacre.

Actually, the grand march (staged on January 18, 1872) was led by Mary Thompson McCook, the first wife of Territorial Governor E.M. McCook. She had risen from her sickbed for the occasion, against the advice of her doctors, but the exertion required to escort the Duke into the ballroom left the poor woman exhausted. Hattie Randolph, Mrs. McCook's predesignated understudy, stepped in for the stricken First Lady and took the Duke's arm for the ceremonial first dance.

during their visit. His master would ensconce himself in an easy chair and spend half an hour or so reminiscing with my father over their early days in the mountains. With his close cropped hair and upright bearing, he was an outstanding figure, and I loved to watch him enter a room, click his heels together, and bow over the ladies' hands. I always longed for the time when I would be old enough for him to do it with me.

This individual was probably Adolf von Schulz (1842-1924), a metallurgist who worked for smelting pioneer Nathaniel Hill in Central City in the late 1860s. He later moved to Denver, became a partner in the chemical laboratory of von Schulz and Low, and was a founding member of the Colorado Scientific Society (1882).

But alas, when I was about to be married, years later during World War I, he came to see us again, a pitiful figure, his shoulders bent, his whole bearing shaken by the impact of the hatred and suspicion that had fallen on him. In his youth he had served his turn in the Imperial German Army, and the stigma of that duty followed him forever. Most of his friends had cast him off.

Our house was one of the few places where he was still welcome. He shook his head as he looked at me. "I am a Hun," he told us bitterly, "and no one cares to have me as a friend anymore." This was virtually true, and in his last illness he was alone and friendless. A Catholic priest did much for him, and everyone felt that "poor old Von" would join the Catholic church before he died, but he clung to his faith. "I was born a Lutheran and shall die a Lutheran," he insisted, and so he did.

Others who often called on Sunday were Colonel Welles and his daughter,

Mrs. Kilham, from across the street. The Colonel, a man with drooping mustaches, had fought for the Union and loved nothing better than to settle himself in a comfortable chair and rehash old campaigns.

With him came his daughter, Mrs. Kilham, a sweet-faced woman with graying blonde hair and baby blue eyes. Mrs. Kilham had been *divorced*. She was the clinging-vine type and had married handsome Fred Kilham, a notorious rake, when she was very young, and lived to regret it. But in that period one married for better or worse, and a woman thought long and hard before she was willing to break the marriage bonds, no matter how intolerable she might find them.

A divorced woman was for some unexplainable reason under a stigma, no matter how blameless she may have been or how blatant her husband's shortcomings. It was her duty to lick her wounds in silence and put up a brave front. A divorcee had to face curious glances and lowered voices, and few women reached the point where they dared risk it.

Where in later years a girl would have gotten herself a job and no doubt in a short time found another husband, since men were as thick as blackberries, Mrs. Kilham returned to the parental roof and lived out her days as companion to her elderly parents. Her trouble was never mentioned, but she always sat pensively in the background,

The Colonel was Ebenezer T. Wells, a former Central City lawyer who served as one of thirty-seven delegates to the state constitutional convention in 1875 and later sat briefly on the state Supreme Court. His daughter, Kitty Wells Kilham, had an advanced education in music but chose not to pursue a performing career, instead marrying Frederick Kilham. The New York-born Kilham came to Denver in 1878 and rose through a series of bank jobs, eventually becoming the president of Western Bank in 1893.

taking little part in the conversation and looking with sad blue eyes at the world that had treated her so ill.

Since I found Mrs. Kilhan's quiet remarks and Colonel Welles' long-winded stories of bygone battles unutterably boring, I was always glad when they took their leave and I would see the Voorhees coming down the street, out for a Sunday stroll. The Voorhees often dropped in for a moment or two. Mrs. Voorhees had been a beautiful widow when Jack Voorhees married her. He was a gallant figure, a Southerner in his early forties with sweeping mustaches, and he had a charming and flattering manner with the ladies.✤

He always wore a frockcoat and silk hat and carried the inevitable gold-headed cane. I always enjoyed their visits, because their talk was light and entertaining, particularly if my sister was present. Mr. Voorhees would tease Ellie and banter with her about her beaux, and there would be funny stories and gay gossip about some party the night before. Often he took me on his knee, told me droll stories, pinched my cheek, and slipped a dime into the pocket of my dress. Some day, he whispered in my ear, I too would grow up to be a belle and have lots of beaux. I doubted this, since I was far from being a beautiful child, but it at least stimulated my self-confidence.

In the evening we usually witnessed an entirely different kind of social gathering:

✤ *Born in Lexington, Kentucky in 1850, John Voorhies came to Colorado in the 1870s and made his fortune in the mines of the San Juan Mountains, then moved to Denver in 1885 and put his wealth into banking and real estate. In his will (he died in 1915), Voorhies left a large sum to the city of Denver for the construction of a monument in Civic Center. The curved row of columns, known as the Voorhies Memorial, still stands on Colfax Avenue just east of the City and County Building—about one block east of the author's childhood home.*

My aunt would invite a group of her intimates for an evening of music. Our house, with its large rooms all opening into each other, was ideally fitted for musicales. There was a large German element in the city, which lived rather clannishly together in one of the older and less fashionable parts of town.

Mr. Thies, the nominal head of the group, was a tall, pleasant-faced German with upstanding hair and kindly blue eyes behind his glasses, and he performed equally well on the violin, viola, or cello. He had his own string quartet, which practiced weekly and played exceptionally well for amateurs. ✥

Around 8 o'clock musicians of various talents would begin arriving, many carrying their black instrument cases, and the house would resound to the strains of Beethoven, Brahms, or Papa Haydn. They would all fiddle away madly, Mr. Thies beating time on the floor with his foot. "Ach, that was bad, very bad. Lightly now, more pianissimo, keep in time, follow me," he would shout, indicating with his bow the place on the music where they should start. Eyes glued to their music racks, bows sawing up and down, faces glistening, they were at it again, the lights of zealots in their eyes.

Sometimes I sat in the parlor watching them, sometimes in the library where my father and mother read, undisturbed by the

✥ *German-born Fritz Thies was one of the West's largest distributors of fine wines and cigars. He also was a first-rate violinist and a tireless champion of Denver's musical development. Thies funded local orchestras, promoted concerts, and organized festivals, while amassing an extraordinary collection of sheet music. He began leading Sunday-night chamber-music sessions in the 1880s and continued to do so until his death in 1921.*

din. Occasionally, my sister would play a violin solo, accompanied by some pianist, or one of Aunt Hattie's star pupils would give a program of songs. Group singing around the piano always topped off the evening, after which they adjourned to the dining room for beer, sandwiches, and welsh rarebit in a chafing dish.

Perhaps this would be rated a dull evening in a more contemporary era, when people have only to flick a dial to hear the world's best orchestras, but it sufficed for us in those benighted days, and they all went home at 11 in a hurly-burly of clanking music racks, snapping instrument cases, hunting of coats and hats, laughter and joking, and the warm glow of good fellowship, good food, and the satisfaction of personal accomplishment.

Firecrackers and a Fall Festival

Two mid-year celebrations brought children to a peak of excitement, exceeded only by the Christmas season. These were the Fourth of July and the annual Festival of Mountain and Plain, observed in the early fall.

The Fourth was not the emasculated affair that children of later generations became accustomed to in the interest of safety and sanity. I well realize that the number of accidents averted over the years by taking the teeth out of the holiday has more than proved the value of caution . But for a third- or fourth-grader, the baby parades and community celebrations can never equal the intoxication of setting off one's first firecracker or laying a piece of punk to an entire package of the tiny Chinese variety.

The day really began the night before. For some unknown reason, the challenge to set off the first explosion of the day made every child eager to spring out of bed when the sun was making its appearance over the horizon.

One year Ruthie, Edmund and I, after much persuasion, finally induced our parents to allow us to spend the night of the third in the little wooden playhouse my father had built in the yard to house our dolls' furniture. With sufficient squeezing, it was possible for the three of us to wedge ourselves in crosswise.

So, wrapped in Navajo blankets, we lay down on the floor and pretended to be the Rover Boys, hunting Indians. The hardness of the boards did not make for easy slumber, and we spent most of the night twisting and turning in an effort to find a soft spot. By 4 A.M. the sun was already coming up, and we crawled stiffly out, washed our faces at the outdoor spigot and, not having removed any of our clothes the night before, were ready for the fray.

Armed with boxes of crackers and pieces of punk, which gave out a delicious Oriental odor, we betook ourselves to the broad horseblock in front of our house and proceeded to salute the day with an enormous cracker. These giant crackers were about the thickness of a man's thumb and twice as long. Tying an extra length of string to the wick, we set it under a tin can, breathlessly applied the punk and scurried out of the way. The resultant noise was pleasurably deafening, and the can sailed high in the air.

Before he gave the world the Hardy Boys, Nancy Drew, and the Bobsey Twins, Edward Stratemeyer created the Rover Boys. These three brothers (Tom, Dick, and Sam) first appeared in 1899 and starred in twenty volumes over the next sixteen years; the Rover Boys' sons continued the saga for an additional ten volumes. In their triumphs over shady and conniving villains, the Rovers exemplifyed "clean living, patriotism, and healthy boyish exuberance."

The Rogers' collie, who had been trailing at our heels, turned and fled howling, his tail between his legs.

We were allowed only one giant cracker. Most were of the two-inch-long variety, which we lit in our hands and tossed into the street. But there were variations, such as a "cat and dog fight." This was effected by breaking two crackers in half, laying the V-shaped wedges opposite each other, and applying a match. They spit, hissed, and jumped about comically.

There were also little brown objects known as worms which, when lit, twisted and wriggled along the sidewalk. Torpedoes made an adequate bang but were considered babyish and used only to startle some unsuspecting grown-up by dropping one covertly on the pavement.

The 1890s witnessed a flourishing of U.S.-manufactured firecrackers and a corresponding decrease in the popularity of Chinese imports. A favorite of the late 1890s was known as the "Dewey battery," named for the U.S. admiral who devastated the Spanish fleet at Manila Bay in 1898.

By 8 A.M. the whole city was thunderously alive. The air resounded to the bark and bang of continual explosions. Now and then a deep-toned boom proclaimed that some enterprising boy had set off a real giant cracker a foot long, often no doubt losing a thumb or finger because some other boy had dared him to hold it in his hands till the very end. Dogs were nowhere to be seen. They had long since fled to the safety of cellars and under porches, where they cowered till the holiday was over.

Milk wagons and delivery trucks were often started by malicious boys who would toss a lighted firecracker right under the horse's nose, while the cursing drivers leaned far out, trying to reach the culprits with their whips. The Fourth could always be counted on for at least one runaway, though fortunately they seldom ended fatally.

One Fourth, hearing a commotion up the street that suggested a runaway, we rushed to look. Down the wide dirt highway came a light wagon, the driver desperately sawing at the reins. The frightened horse was running at a mad gallop. The street cleared instantaneously. People scrambled for the sidewalk, and mothers snatched their children out of reach of the wildly flying hoofs. Men ran out and waved their arms in an attempt to stop the terrified animal but only succeeded in frightening him further. The wagon swerved violently and overturned while we watched in fascinated horror. Would the driver be caught in the reins and dragged? Luckily, he rolled free of the cart, which hurtled down the street for another few blocks. A man finally brought the horse to bay by flinging himself at the bridle and bringing the animal to a quivering halt. The driver, his face scratched and bloody, got up, dusted himself off, and walked stiffly toward his buggy. We returned to our crackers.

Later in the morning came the parade. It was practically the same parade that took place Decoration Day, when floral tributes were placed on veterans' graves, but people enjoyed parades, and the veterans were

Then as now, fireworks ignited delight and dismay in equal measure. Accidents killed several hundred Americans (primarily children) each July 4 and injured several thousand, leading critics to dub it "Death's Busiest Day." On July 5, the Rocky Mountain News would publish the names of all those killed or maimed— "Fifty-five Victims to Fireworks is Colorado's Sacrifice on the Alter of Patriotism," read a typical headline. Local officials lived in dread that a fireworks-induced blaze would ravage the city, and many retailers refused to stock fireworks for that very reason. But the demand never flagged, and it inevitably got met.

always ready to dress up in their worn uniforms for the benefit of the admiring citizenry. We lived close enough to downtown to hear the bands and to run for Fifteenth Street the minute the sound of drums rolled in the distance.

First marched a squadron of police in their heavy helmets, their long wooden clubs protruding from their belts. Behind them came Cook's Drum Corps, a sizable outfit of half-grown boys, their bright Zouave uniforms and instruments furnished by a philanthropic citizen named George Cook. They took pride in their group, practiced continually, and marched well, and their gay colors and thunderous tattoos made them in demand for every parade.

A company of soldiers recently returned from the war in the Philippines generally made up the next contingent. The khaki-clad riders in broad-brimmed hats were greeted with uproarious applause as their sleek horses clattered by. ❧

Then came the Civil War veterans, wearing the forage caps and blue uniforms of the Union Army. Most had served in the Colorado regiments that had fought the war in the West, but there were many who had belonged in various eastern corps and taken part on many a bloody battlefield.

A large banner, stretching across the entire street, heralded the crux of the parade. In letters a foot high the banner proclaimed "Veterans of Shiloh." These were the elite,

❧ *Denver showed its Spanish-American War veterans far more appreciation than most other U.S. communities. The city paid for a special train to bring the First Colorado Voluntary Infantry Regiment home from San Francisco (where the troops were mustered out), then drew 75,000 citizens to a parade for them on September 14, 1899. This group of veterans played a major role in founding the nationwide Veterans of Foreign Wars (VFW).*

the heroes, the immortals. With their torn battle flags streaming in the morning breeze, the bearers sweating under the July sun, they stepped out proudly to the cheers of the crowd. Most were elderly men now. Some limped along on peglegs or crutches; dozens had empty sleeves. Scattered among their ranks were several who wore the Rebel gray. These always received an equal ovation with the Blue marchers. There was little bitterness here in the West such as marked the aftermath of the war in the East. Most of these men had fought Indians on the plains with the U.S. Cavalry after the war, and we recognized many familiar faces.

In the evening, of course, came fireworks. We were only allowed Roman candles or sparklers, since rockets had a way of backfiring into the face of the sender and were also very expensive. So, after our own supply was exhausted, we climbed up to the roof to see what we could of the municipal display at City Park.

Enthusiasm for public fireworks displays reached an apex in the Victorian age, as advances in the pyrotechnic arts gave rise to a spate of spectacular shows. On July 4, 1901 (when the author was ten), one of the largest displays in history lit up Pikes Peak—a massive petroleum-fueled bonfire that shot a pillar of flame nearly a thousand feet above the summit. The sight thrilled crowds in Denver and was visible as far away as Cheyenne, Wyoming.

My father opened the trap door that led from a ladder-like staircase in the big unfinished attic, and we emerged on a small square platform on top of the house. It was a tight squeeze for six camp chairs, and it was extremely dirty, but once ensconced there, what a thrill to look grandly down three stories watching the passers-by on the street below. By 11 it was all over.

The sky was dark once more, and only a few belated explosions broke the customary stillness of the night. The Fourth was over for another year, and we were only too glad to creep exhausted into bed.

In the clear, crisp autumn days, Denver celebrated the winning of the West with an annual pageant known as the Festival of Mountain and Plain. To us children, this had all the elements of a first-class week-long circus, plus the advantage of having events in which we could participate. The affair was started by a group of business-men calling themselves the "Slaves of the Silver Serpent," whose identities for some reason were supposed to be kept a dark secret. It was patterned after the New Or-leans Mardi Gras, though on a less grandi-ose scale, and while it lacked the panoply and tradition of the larger city's celebration, for a small community it did very well and had a true western flavor all its own.

It started the first of the week with a monster parade. Indians from all the nearby reservations were invited, and they came in droves. Many lived in tepees down by the banks of the Platte, where one could go and stare at them, as we did occasionally.

To a child these people looked peaceable, and it was hard to believe, peering down from the safety of the viaduct at the sprawl-ing cantonment with squaws boiling kettles over campfires and braves lolling among the cottonwood trees, that only a few years ago these people had been considered the dreaded scourge of the plains.

Launched in 1895, the Festival of Mountain and Plain was designed to promote Colorado's vast resources—and thereby help Denver recover from the effects of the Silver Panic of 1893. The inaugural event featured a "Pageant of Progress" that traced Colorado history from the ancient puebloans of the Mesa Verde region through the pioneer era right up to the present, with a nod toward the expecta-tions of Denver's future greatness.

The parade consisted mostly of floats signifying the early days of the community: covered wagons with girls in dresses of the 1840s and 1850s, buckskinned miners with pick and shovel, Buffalo Bill with his riders. All the old stagecoaches were taken out of mothballs, and they rattled along the streets filled with men in slouch hats and dress of the Civil War period.

The Indians came next, tall painted warriors in the full glory of war paint and feathers, the chiefs striding impassively along, the squaws following meekly behind, their papooses strapped to their backs. At the end of the procession came the Silver Serpent, a huge glittering reptile whose elongated body was stretched over the heads of twenty or more men as it writhed and twisted up the street.

Friday afternoon there was a bronco-busting contest at the corner of Colfax and Broadway. This was one of the city's busiest intersections, across from the Capitol grounds, but at that time there was a vacant lot on one corner owned by one of the city's wealthiest magnates and kept as a pasture for a lonely Jersey cow, which meditatively chewed its cud and supplied milk for the infant daughter of the family. But during the festival week the cow was removed, a grandstand was put up, and the lot was transformed into a battleground where the huskiest cowboys off the ranges pitted their skill against the toughest, meanest broncos

The lot, on the northeast corner of Colfax and Broadway, was owned by pioneer banker, railroad builder, and water developer Walter Cheesman. The cow belonged to one of Cheesman's neighbors.

that could be found throughout all the
ranches of Colorado and Wyoming. ❧

One who has never witnessed a real old-
fashioned bronco-busting contest with
skilled performers has missed the thrill of a
lifetime. It combines the excitement of a
football game and a bullfight without the
bloodshed and the cruelty of the latter.
The stands are filled with gaily dressed
people, the sky is dazzlingly blue, pennants
flutter in the stiff breeze, and bands blare
loudly as the governor and his staff enter
their box. Cowboys, magnificent in their
finest regalia, strut ostentatiously about
the arena. The very air is charged with life,
color, excitement. The wiry little ponies are
led in, manes tossing, eyes rolling, hoofs
lashing out wildly. One is singled out, and
strong hands blindfold him and force him
to the ground, then lace a saddle on his
unwilling back. A cowboy comes forward,
straddles the prostrate horse and larrups
it with his quirt as the men leap out of
the way. The maddened animal, goaded to
fury by the rowelling spurs, struggles to
his feet as the blindfold is unloosed. Back
and forth across the arena he plunges, snort-
ing, kicking, rearing, trying every trick he
knows to dislodge this unwelcome burden
while the crowd shrieks encouragement.

"Yiiiiiipppppeeee, ride him cowboy!"

Ride him he does for a brief minute. Then
the pony shies violently, makes a series of
frantic bounds high in the air, and comes

❧ *The Festival of Mountain
and Plain featured a rodeo
just once, in 1901. Billed
as the "Rough Riders
Tournament," it was such
a great success that
organizers staged it again
in 1902, even though the
Festival proper was
cancelled. The 1902
contest saw 1901 champion
Thad Sowder defend his
title, although a judging
scandal tainted the
achievement. Sowder's
victory, whether legitmate or
not, brought him $500, a
silver "world champion's"
belt, and a contract to
perform in Buffalo Bill's
Wild West Show.*

down rigid, his legs as taut and stiff as steel rods. The rider catapults from the saddle and lies prostrate in the dirt. A gasp goes up from the crowd. Is he killed? No, he's only stunned. He finally gets to his feet and walks off grinning as the pony, free from his unwelcome burden, shakes his mane and trots toward the gate.

One after another the horses are led out and saddled, one after another the riders are flung ignominiously into the dirt, and the whole performance begins over again. Back and forth across the arena they battle, man against horse, until eventually some tall lean cowboy, his mouth set grimly, manages to stay on his mount until the animal, limp, exhausted, and quivering, stands motionless and conquered. The cowboy dismounts, pats the horse, and leads him out by the bridle to the roars of the onlookers. Cowgirls, trick riders, comedy teams, and cavalrymen from a nearby post also help to fill out the afternoon programs.

That evening there was a great ball, with one of the current belles of the city being crowned as Queen of the Silver Serpent. ❧ My sister went, of course, but since I was too young, I was allowed instead to take part in the Saturday afternoon masquerade, when everyone turned out in costume, mingling on the streets in a grand free-for-all. This event lasted far into the next morning, with much hijinks and drunken revelry. However, Ruthie, Edmund, and I

❧ *The* Denver Post, *the Festival's major sponsor, dropped names profusely during its coverage of the annual ball, yet the Young family merited only one mention—in 1899, when a gossip columnist spotted Eleanor Young at the society ball hobnobbing with various notables in the private box of department-store mogul William Cooke Daniels. The highly cultured Youngs likely*

had been permitted to go provided we were safely home before dark.

Unfortunately, my mother had neglected to think of a costume for me in advance, and a last-minute search through the trunks in the attic failed to produce anything small enough for me to wear. However, she finally unearthed a pair of short black satin pants, which had belonged to a page's costume Aunt Hattie had once worn in opera.

"These aren't very much too big," my mother said, as she pinned them with safety pins to my Ferris waist. "But you must be careful of them. This was a very expensive little costume."

Over this, horror of horrors, I wore an old flannel bedjacket, forever associated in my mind with bouts of measles, chicken pox, and whooping cough.

With a Mexican sombrero on my head, I was considered ready for the occasion. Well, I thought after one look at myself, no one will know me anyway with a mask on. I hurried out to join Ruthie and Edmund, who both were garbed in real Indian costume. They looked askance at my curious get-up but were polite enough not to comment on it, and we made off up the street toward Broadway, where we could hear bands playing. Crowds were beginning to swarm all over the streets, clad in every conceivable costume. People were milling back and forth, throwing confetti, squirting water pistols, and indulging in various

found little of interest among the Festival's rather prosaic attractions. Most of those in the Youngs' circle of friends were similarly absent from Festival events; the Thatchers, Rogerses, McCourts, Tabors, and others made token appearances at the society ball but otherwise seem to have kept their distance. The author is mistaken in her recollection of a Saturday revel; the masquerade always took place on a Thursday, the last day of the three-day Festival.

kinds of horseplay. A man turned his water pistol on us, soaking us to the skin. We skirted the edge of the crowd, holding hands, munching popcorn, and watching the fun.

As the afternoon waned, more and more paraders streamed in, and the gaiety which up to now had been good-natured pranks became more and more boisterous. The police were beginning to have trouble keeping the crowd in check. A band started up playing "There'll Be a Hot Time in the Old Town Tonight." ❧ With that the crowd, with one accord, took up the tune and, singing and yelling, started to march toward Seventeenth Street.

In spite of ourselves, we were caught up in the tide and swirled along with it. We tried to keep together but were penned in among big, heavy, sweating bodies, and the breath was almost knocked out of us. My hat was torn off and trampled on, and I lost hold of Ruthie completely. I was swept along in the melee, pushed and shoved between two burly men dressed as miners. Finally the crowd parted enough so that I managed to elbow my way under their arms, squeezing between their legs, and eventually got to the edge of the sidewalk, hatless and breathless.

I looked around frantically for Ruthie and Edmund, but they were nowhere to be seen. Suddenly I saw two red devils bearing down on me.

"Hey kid, are you a boy or a girl?"

❧ *"Hot Time" is one of the most durable compositions in U.S. history. Theodore Metz wrote the melody in 1886 (though some musicologists believe he stole it from a piano player in a St. Louis brothel), and Joe Hayden added the lyrics in 1896. Two years later, Teddy Roosevelt's Rough Riders supposedly sang "Hot Time" during their famous charge up San Juan Hill. The song retained its currency during World War I and, as late as the 1930s, was still familiar enough to serve as the jingle for Warner Bros.' Looney Tunes cartoons.*

One of them made a grab for me. He was swaying unsteadily, and I could smell the whiskey on his breath. Terrified, I jerked away from him and started to run. The second one reached out and grabbed the back of my pants. There was a ripping sound, the pins gave way, and the pants slid to the sidewalk, revealing me in my short, white drawers. The men roared with laughter. ✥

Leaving my pants behind me on the sidewalk, I shudderingly darted away up the street faster than I had ever run in my life. I could still feel those clutching hands, smell that liquory breath. At the end of the block, completely winded, I paused to look back. They hadn't come after me, but in the gathering dusk I could still see them circling around a lamppost, waving my pants in the air. I was thankful for the darkness and devoutly hoped no one would see me shamelessly walking on a public thoroughfare in my underdrawers. I was sure I was in for a scolding, too, for having stayed out so late, and for losing Aunt Hattie's nice satin pants. Soon the lights of our house shone out across the street. Welcome sight! I saw my father open the front door and come out on the porch.

"Here she is now," I heard him call as I came panting up the steps. "Good gracious child, where have you been? I was just coming out to look for you. Mr. Rollins arrived from Boston this afternoon and is having dinner with us. He's in the library

✥ This type of criminal behavior was a perennial concern during the Festival, particularly at the closing-day masquerade, when as many as 250,000 people (a large share of them drunk) packed the streets of downtown. Professional pickpockets traveled in from out of state just for the occasion, forcing the police to beef up their downtown forces—and commensurately to dilute their patrols everywhere else. As a result, Denver inevitably suffered a spate of residential break-ins and burglaries during the Festival.

now. Your mother wants you to go upstairs and get cleaned up for dinner. The Clarys will be here, too."

He hadn't even noticed that I was wet, hatless, and pantless! I thanked Heaven for the advent of Mr. Rollins, who was or had been my father's partner and often dropped into town unexpectedly but usually came to us for dinner. With him here, maybe no one would inquire too fully about the masquerade or want to know what had become of my costume, or I would never be allowed to go again. Perhaps Mr. Rollins might even invite me to visit them on their New Hampshire farm, as I was always fervently hoping he would do.

I scurried through the hall and up the back stairs. Safe at last in my lttle room, I stripped off my wet clothes. This time luck had been with me.

I kept very quiet during dinner, listening to the grown-up conversation, and no one questioned me about the masquerade. As we all sat in the library after dinner, the doorbell rang and, Mary being occupied, my father opened it.

I heard him talking to someone, and it sounded like Ruthie's voice. Presently he came back into the room, looking puzzled.

"Ruthie said she found something that she thinks belongs to you," he said, addressing himself to me. "She and Edmund came along Court Place and saw it on the side-

*"Mr. Rollins" was Edward W. Rollins, Frank Young's primary business partner. The son of E.H. Rollins (a former U.S. Senator and high-placed Union Pacific official), he was born in New Hampshire in 1850 and came to Colorado in 1871 as a construction engineer on the Colorado Central Railway. In 1876 he moved to Denver and launched a securities brokerage; Young joined the firm in 1880 and became a partner in 1881. When his father died in 1889, Rollins inherited a great fortune and moved back east to manage it, leaving Young (by then vice president of Rollins Investment Company) in charge of his extensive Colorado interests.

walk. I told her that I was sure she was mistaken."

He held up to view a dirty, sodden object. My mother was eyeing it with distaste. "No, of course it doesn't belong to us," she said positively. "Throw it away."

He turned toward the door again. Red with mortification, I started after him. "Wait, papa, wait. It is mine," I gulped. "I'm sorry. It's ...it's Aunt Hattie's black satin pants."

Christmas

Of all the times in the year, the one we children looked forward to most was the Christmas season. We used to start talking about it as far ahead as September. Often I would wake up in the early morning and steal into my parents' bed, snuggle down between them, and say, "Now let's talk about Christmas."

It was not that we gave or received a multiplicity of gifts in the extravagant fashion that later developed, nor did the holiday possess a particularly commercialized atmosphere. The stores rarely pictured Christmas goods until two or three weeks before, so that excitement remained at a high pitch. Christmas didn't come as an anti-climax; the decorations did not go up before Thanksgiving, as would be the custom in later years, and so the symbols did not lose their meaning and freshness long before Christmas ever arrived.

The two things I always wanted most were books and a new dress for my doll. Ruthie and I each had a doll with which we played for years, far past the age at which most children put them away. We considered these dolls—mine named Bea, hers called Mamie—to be living people. We invented families for them. We followed their activities through babyhood, girlhood, marriage, and childbirth, much as soap operas carry on episode after episode. Our dolls went to school and blossomed into young ladyhood, with beaux and parties.

We camped with them in a tent in the Rogers's yard, went to Europe with them, and saw them through exciting adventures and hairbreadth escapes. We made their clothes and wrote plays for them. They were battered and broken over the years, their wigs replaced many times and the cracks mended in their bisque faces. But no other dolls would ever have been the same. ❧

One Christmas my mother gave me a new doll, which lay for weeks in its gaudy attire in its box, untouched. Mother finally gave it to the washwoman's little girl. After that she made new clothes for Bea but never again attempted to substitute a new doll.

Another thing I wanted dreadfully was a bicycle. Both Ruth and Edmund had bicycles, and if I had one we could ride back and forth to school, take our lunch, and go on picnics to the edge of town perhaps, or anyway as far as City Park, where there

❧ *Most bisque dolls of that era were imported from Germany. In the United States, the most popular German brand was Kestner, distributed through Sears & Roebuck; other German doll manufacturers included Kammer and Reinhardt and Simon & Halbig. One U.S. firm, Fulpers, did make bisque dolls, though it did not specialize in them.*

were lovely broad stretches of lawn on which to picnic and a lake where you could get a boat ride for ten cents.

It always snowed early in the high mountains, so I always associated snow with Christmas. A Christmas without snow would have been unthinkable.

Snow began often in October and sometimes lay on the ground until April. But the sun came out quickly afterwards and the weather would be cold, clear, and sparkling, with the snow heaped high along the walks. As soon as the stores held Christmas things, we children were sometimes allowed to go downtown alone to buy our presents and to gaze enraptured in the store windows. To go on the afternoon of Christmas Eve was the greatest thrill of all.

Newspapers of the era reveal a Christmas season not much different from today's. Charity drives, concerts, parades, and the last-minute rush at the post office provided fodder for mid-December editions, then as now. Likewise, advertisements grew larger and more urgent as the shopping days dwindled, and prices decreased commensurately, as retailers hustled to move unsold merchandise.

The snow would generally be falling thickly—great fat flakes that seemed imbued with the jollity of the season, so merrily did they dance and whirl through the air. Everywhere was gaeity and laughter, and great crowds of people filling the sidewalks, their arms full of bundles, good-naturedly pushing and jostling each other and calling out "Merry Christmas" to everybody.

There were no automobiles, and not many carriges ventured out. The only street traffic consisted of a few delivery wagons and people walking in the streets and on the walks, ankle deep in snow. Our doorbell rang incessantly—messenger boys handing in presents for Aunt Hattie from admirers and pupils, florists' wagons delivering great bunches of American Beauty roses for my sister, an errand boy with a belated gift from the store, hastily smuggled into the house and upstairs before I could see it. I would hear the hum of my mother's sewing machine as she finished some last minute handiwork, probably for my doll, with the door tightly closed.

There were no Santa Clauses then on every corner and in every shop window to confuse and disenchant youngsters. Santa came on one evening only, and that was Christmas Eve. I knew because I saw him every year. He always came first to the Rogers' house before he started his long trek across the country.

The Rogerses celebrated Christmas with dinner and a tree the night before, instead of in the morning as we did. They invited all their relatives and close friends to dinner, including all the children, and old and young mixed happily in a hospitable home blazing with log fires and radiating warmth and cheer. Ages ranged from old Grandma Blood, who was ninety-one, to the three little Burritts, who were younger even than Ruthie, Edmund, and me. The table—which stretched the length of the dining room, straight through the sitting room, and into the parlor—held the mammoth turkey at one end, while a smiling Japanese boy hired for the occasion carried to the other a roast suckling pig, with a rosy apple in its

The Santa Claus legend was still emerging during the author's childhood; she and her sister were probably the first generation of Youngs to grow up believing in Santa. For example, his red costume didn't appear until the mid-1880s, and other particulars of Santa culture—his North Pole abode, work force of elves, even the pot belly and Ho! Ho! Ho! tagline—did not crystallize until well into the twentieth century.

mouth. So lifelike was it I could scarcely bear to eat it, but once one had overcome this hurdle it was crisp, juicy, and tender. After we had stuffed our way through the first course and a flaming plum pudding decked with holly, there would come a mysterious stamping and clanking on the side porch and a knock at the long French windows.

Someone would rush to open the door and admit Santa in his red suit and cap, his whiskers white with snow. He would snatch up the smallest child present and seat her or him on his shoulder, and the parade to the third floor would begin. Unlike our house, where the attic was a big, unfinished cavern in whose dark corners under the eaves lurked all kinds of indescribable terrors to my childish mind, the Rogers' third floor had been converted into one huge playroom with many windows, a hardwood floor, plastered walls, and even an upright piano in one corner. As we flung open the door, there in all its glittering splendor towered the tree, its top branches sweeping the ceiling and hung with pink popcorn balls, candy canes, and bright-colored paper chains. Dozens of small candles instead of electric lights gave it a soft radiance; far more hazardous than subsequent methods, but still lovely.

Dr. Gower, a musician of renown and organist at St. John's Cathedral, sat down at the piano and thundered out a lively march. Everyone joined hands and danced

A descendant of Sir Walter Scott, John H. Gower was born in England in 1855. This musical prodigy was the youngest person in a century to earn a doctorate of music from

around the tree, singing and shouting. Three times we circled it, and then the children fell to on the popcorn and candy, as well as the toys scattered about the foot. A small electric train ran around the base—we had electric trains even then, though they were not as complicated nor as efficient as those of today. Instead of plugging in a switch, you had to put two cathodes in water to start the current. But it ran just the same.

At 11 o'clock, an unheard-of hour for me, I was called home, surfeited with food and excitement, my arms full of presents. After the noise and heat of the party, it was wonderful to come out into the cold, clear night air. The snow had stopped falling, and the sky was brilliant with stars as only a Colorado sky can be. An unearthly hush filled the night, broken only by distant carollers walking their rounds. In our hall the lights were low, but the fire in the big fireplace burned cheerfully. The coals glowed and twinkled. For some reason we never had a tree. We hung up our stockings instead, and there were five strung along the banister at the foot of the staircase—my father's ample sock, my thin ribbed stocking, and the respectable, black thin lisle stockings of my mother, sister, and aunt. Aunt Hattie's stockings always had a white heel and toe— three for a dollar, the best quality.

I stole quickly upstairs, too excited to sleep. Had I not seen Santa himself, and had he not assured me that he would stop at our

Oxford, and at age eleven he received a personal appointment from Queen Victoria as the organist at Windsor Castle. He moved to Denver in 1887 at the behest of Dean Hart, a fellow Briton and director of St. John's Cathedral (which then stood at Welton and Twentieth Streets). Dr. Gower's spiritual expertise went far beyond religious music: He also was a world-renowned authority on psychic phenomena. After Gower's death in 1922, various people reported having ghostly contact with him.

house next? I was not fooled when I woke up the next morning, for there were the stockings filled and running over.

As the years went by, I realized there was no Santa Claus, but I was never rudely disillusioned, and the enchantment still lingered. There sat Beatrice, my doll, on the sofa, magnificent in a new dress, a new coat and bonnet, and even a little handbag, her cracked and battered face beaming over her new attire. I drew a long breath. There, red and gleaming against the wall, stood a bicycle—the newest girls' model. I looked at it with awe, touching the smooth leather saddle, the pedals, the shining wheels. Now I, too, could take off to school in the morning and not have to go by myself on the streetcar.

Our Christmas dinner, always served at 2 o'clock, was a sedate affair compared with the boisterous jollity of the night before. My two girl cousins usually came to dinner, as well as any of our family friends who had no place to go. After dinner there were usually more callers, or I would go out with Aunt Hattie to deliver some belated gift, skipping along with my doll in my arms.

The evening was quiet, but it was good to come in out of the cold to the glow of the fire; to lie on the big bearskin rug with my pile of new books beside me, clamoring to be read. Yes, of all days, Christmas was the best, I thought as I fell asleep, my doll hugged tight to my bosom.

Bicycling's incredible popularity in the 1890s spawned about three hundred bicycle manufacturers across the United States. None appears to have been located in Denver, but the city did have an authorized dealer of Victor bicycles, the brand credited with launching the craze and one of the nation's best-selling makes. Another top seller, Columbia, also was readily available in Denver, as was the upstart Schwinn New World Bicycle, which appeared in 1895.

Housekeeping and Hospitality

We had a large house. In a later era it no doubt would have been put up for sale or converted to apartments because of the scarcity of household help, as well as the expense of running it. However, a moderately well-off family like ours could reasonably afford two or three helpers. Most of our friends employed at least two maids, and usually a gardener or coachman. We ourselves had no horses or carriages, and this was a source, I think, of great chagrin to my mother at times, for she had reached the age when most of her friends rode sedately about in carriages or Victorias and rarely condescended to use the streetcars. But my father's business affairs had taken a turn for the worse by then, and he was cutting expenses wherever possible.

There was really no "servant problem," although this was, as always, a favorite topic for discussion among housewives. If our cook left, we could always replace her inside of a few hours by calling the employment agency, and another tall, gaunt Swede would stalk into the kitchen, march up to the third floor, remove her hat, and ask us if we wanted lemon pie for dinner.

The two fixtures who remained almost throughout my childhood were Binnie, the cook, born and raised on an Iowa farm, and Irish-born Mary, straight from County Cork, who arrived to try the place and stayed sixteen years, until my father died and our household was broken up. Mary had curly black hair and red cheeks and was as clean and neat as a new pin. Every afternoon she donned her black frock, with its immaculate white collar, cuffs, and apron, and was available to answer the door till 10 P.M. She had one afternoon off a week, which meant that she could leave the house about 2 and return to serve dinner at 6:30. She did, however, have every other Sunday off, which was more than most maids did, and she saved enough out of her modest salary to give a good part of her earnings to her sister, who had married a policeman and raised a large family.

Twice a week came Freda, the large, rawboned German woman who did the washing and heavy cleaning. Removing her battered felt hat, she would disappear down the cellar steps into the dark, subterranean rooms that held the laundry tubs and the maids' watercloset. Sometimes I

Most European immigrants, such as Irish-born Mary in the kitchen and German-born Freda doing the washing, found that the only jobs open to them were in menial labor and domestic service. Although the level of

94

went down there to talk to her as, elbow-deep in suds, she scrubbed up and down, up and down on the washboard. The cellar always had a hot, steamy smell due, of course, to the huge boiler of clothes; cooking away on the little coal stove. The next day the stove heated the army of irons, which for some reason Freda always referred to as "sad" irons. I never knew why, but thought it might be because she was sad at having so much underwear to launder. With three women and a child in the house, there were great piles of ruffled petticoats, lacy chemises, white cotton drawers, corset covers, and shirtwaists all in a white, sweet-smelling heap in the basket.

Freda would take up one of the irons from the stove and test it with her wet finger, making a hissing noise. "Chust right," she would say, running her arm across her forehead, which was moist with sweat. "Vatch now vile ve make your dress nice and pretty." And I would watch breathlessly while the iron made a beautiful, smooth swath down the well-starched gingham. When Freda had finished the ironing she did the cleaning, scrubbing the cellar steps from top to bottom, and when she was through at the end of the day she looked so tired. I was so sorry that she had to walk all the way home, far down Colfax Avenue under the viaduct, which was the poorer section of the city, though Denver had no real slums.

discrimination against them was far less than what Asian and Hispanic immigrants faced, Europeans often found themselves at odds with Americans due to religious differences.

"Mrs. Potts' Cold Handle Sad Irons" appeared in 1871 and became ubiquitous in U.S. and European households. Invented by Mary Florence Potts of Iowa, their innovation was the detachable handle; as an iron cooled off, the user removed the handle and transferred it to another iron waiting on the stove. The term "sad" in this context meant "heavy" or "compact" (a now obsolete definition).

Outdoors our old colored man, Leviathan (pronounced Lee-*vee*-aythan) Stark, mowed the lawn, tended the furnace, and in winter shoveled snow. ❧ The Sullivans, on the other end of the block, also employed a colored man, who was their coachman and took excellent care of the horses, which were housed in the stable across the alley back of our house. Leslie was a shambling old man, given to muttering to himself about his work and not terribly fond of children. When Ruthie, Edmund, and I occasionally ran up and down the alley, he would be lounging near the door and would call out, "If youse chillun dass come near my horses, I'll come after you with my whip."

This was, of course, enough to challenge us to venturing as close as we dared to the building, calling him to "come out and get us." He would be hiding behind the stable door and would lunge out suddenly, cracking a long blacksnake whip. It whistled over our heads but never actually touched us, while we ran for dear life.

While we waged constant warfare with Leslie and never missed an opportunity to heckle and badger him, our taunts never carried the slightest taint of ethnic prejudice or any jibes concerning his color. It was merely the reaction of mischievous children to the whims and grudges of a cantankerous old man. Negroes were accepted into the daily life of Denver with less bigotry than in any city of its size I ever knew. ❧

❧ The terms "colored" and "Negro" were, of course, considered appropriate (even polite) in the 1890s—and were still common in the 1960s, when the author wrote this memoir.

❧ Which is not to say that African-Americans in Victorian Denver did not encounter bigotry. On the contrary, discrimination against them increased

Twice a year there occurred what might have been termed the dressmaking marathon. This lasted a week or more and took place in what was then known as the spare room. It was really the guest room, but since guests were a rare occurrence, the furniture was usually shrouded in sheets. It was a large, sunny room with a flowered Brussels carpet and shiny green furniture. There was even a little basin with running water in the corner, surrounded by a Chinese screen. The sheets were put on the floor and the dressmaker's dummy hauled down from the attic and installed in the middle of the room. Mrs. Tracy and Miss Carr arrived to stay all day, eat lunch with the family, and take over the sewing for the various feminine wardrobes.

Miss Carr was a mild, gentle soul who rarely spoke, but Mrs. Tracy was a pert little vixen with darting black eyes and a sharp temper. She was quick and clever at her work, and as she sat at the machine, she stitched away swiftly, and expertly, and almost angrily, I thought, as if the rapid treading allowed her to rid herself of unwelcome emotions. She felt very deeply on certain subjects, principally politics. My father and all his friends were staunch Republicans, just as they were loyal Episcopalians, Presbyterians, or Congregationalists. At times, there was much talk going on about the Democratic and Populist leader, Mr. William Jennings Bryan,

during this era. Jim Crow laws introduced in the 1890s prohibited Denver's black residents (who numbered about four thousand) from buying property in most sections of town; restricted their access to public parks, hotels, restaurants, and theaters; and raised barriers to employment and education. Thus excluded, African-Americans developed their own businesses and social institutions, building a thriving community centered in the Five Points neighborhood.

and his persistent efforts to be president. One afternoon, I overheard Mrs. Tracy and Miss Carr wrangling over the candidates. Mrs. Tracy's face was turkey red.

"Are you going to vote for Bryan or McKinley?" I asked her curiously.

Her eyes snapped. The machine was whirring ominously. "Neither—I'm a Socialist," she announced tartly.

I stared at her in horror. If she had confessed to being a cannibal, I could scarcely have been more shocked. A socialist? Why, socialists were nearly the same as anarchists, whom I thought of as bearded men who threw bombs at royalty and were exiled to Siberia in chains. I wondered if my father knew about this and whether it was safe to have her in the house. I told my father afterward, and he only laughed; but I never felt at ease with Mrs. Tracy after that.

Imagine young Elizabeth's unease had she realized that Denver in the 1890s was teeming with "radical" elements. The city's large population of immigrant laborers made it a hotbed of working-class activism, which was further inflamed by the Silver Panic of 1893. The hard-line Western Federation of Miners had a large local presence, as did Jacob Coxey's "Poor People's Army" and left-wing political organizations such as the Union Labor Party, the People's Party, and the Populists. In 1892 Colorado elected a Populist governor, Davis Waite; ten years later

I always enjoyed being in the spare room while a sewing bee was going on, however. It was full of laughter and gossip and people coming and going. It was my job to collect the bright pieces of material that fell on the floor and put them into a large canvas bag, known as the "piece bag." My mother, who was a fine sewer, was turning all these scraps into a patchwork quilt. This engrossed her for several years, as all the little pieces of various shapes and sizes were set in with exquisite feather stitching. She worked on it night after night in the library while my father read.

My mother was an excellent house-keeper, and there were two tasks which she would delegate to no one. One was washing the pink Venetian glass chandelier in the parlor, which took place once a year and occupied an entire morning. Mary, her head wrapped in a towel, stood on a step-ladder and handed the pieces down to my mother, who washed them with great care. Each piece was numbered, and after being washed and dried had to be gotten back into its proper slot. I thought this the greatest amount of wasted effort and vowed I would never have anything like it if ever I had a house, though I have to admit the effect afterwards was really dazzling.

I had no hand in this business, but as soon as I was old enough I was always pressed into service as soon to help with pinning down the heavy net window curtains—a job I hated. There were at least twelve pairs in the house, all starched so stiffly they would almost stand alone. They were edged with tape, stitched on in little pointed triangles. Every curtain had to be pinned to the car-pet on a sheet, and each little point had to be pulled out and pinned down on a line drawn by yardstick. This job also took hours, and one emerged with aching knees and a thumb permanently punctured from pushing in the heads of pins.

I hated housecleaning time anyway, with the carpets all up and Leviathan beat-ing away at them in the yard with a heavy

(when the author was twelve) an unabashed Socialist, David Coates, ascended to the lieutenant governorship.

rattan beater. My father hated it, too, and always stayed at the office as long as possible during this week. I was often called on to run errands or help in small jobs, but I escaped through the fence to the Rogers house whenever possible and stayed in hiding, hoping no one would find me.

But parties were fun. Every now and then my parents or my sister would give a dinner party. This always meant extra help, usually the Negro cateress, Jane Vernell, who arrived at 10 in the morning to get everything ready. Binnie was demoted to the role of kitchen maid, and Mrs. Vernell took over the supervision of the menu. Dinners were no such informal, easy affairs as later became the practice. Dinners at our house were occasionally for twenty people at a time. Mary and Leviathan would drag the large round tabletop up from the cellar, dust it off, and put it on top of the dining room table. The best gold-banded china and glass was taken out and washed.

Jane Vernell continued a long tradition of African-American success in Denver's restaurant and catering industries. It began with Barney Ford, the ex-slave who ran one of frontier Denver's most prominent inns. Oliver Touissant Jackson, famous as the founder of the African-American farming colony of Dearfield, made his name and fortune as Denver's leading caterer in the 1880s. When Jackson

Jane Vernell's dinners had at least five and often six courses—generally a clear soup, a fish course, then a crown roast of lamb with little paper drawers on the ends of the chops, or maybe a tenderloin of beef. I believe sherbert came next, then a fame and a salad and, finally, tutti-frutti ice cream. I was allowed to stay in the kitchen during the preparations, provided I didn't bother anyone. "Keep out of the way, child," someone would be sure to say, and I would hastily scamper under the kitchen table, from which vantage point I could watch the proceedings with interest. At 7 in the evening Mary would come flying down into the kitchen, her cheeks like peonies, hurriedly tying her apron to be ready to answer the door.

One night about this time, when all the family were upstairs dressing and no one was looking, I slipped into the dining room to take a peek at the table. It was all in readiness, even to the place cards, lettered in my father's beautiful script. In the center of the white damask tablecloth was the beautiful French compote my mother had brought from Paris, flanked on either side by the gold and white candelabra, which held six or eight candles with pink shades. At each place was a glittering array of wine glasses. The candles cast a soft pink glow on the table. It looked like a fairyland setting to me. I stood admiring it and finally reached over and helped myself to a large, flat, pink mint from a nearby plate.

Hearing a footstep in the hall, I quickly ducked under the tablecloth, which came nearly to the floor. Kitty, a red-haired maid I didn't like, since she had a sharp temper and didn't care much for children, came into the room and started filling the water glasses.

I stayed carefully in my hiding place, nibbling my mint. It was dark and cozy in there, very much like a tent, and I pretended I was

moved to Boulder in 1894, Vernell stepped into his niche and remained there for most of the next quarter-century, becoming prominent enough in business to land on various bank and church boards. She died in 1922.

101

❧ *Jane Andrews published* The Seven Little Sisters Who Live on the Round Ball That Floats in the Air *in 1888. The book, a series of loosely related stories, illustrates the lives of children in the Far East, Africa, Europe, and beyond. Gemila, the Child of the Desert, lives in a tent in the Sahara and describes the wondrous creatures and beautiful sights of that part of the world.*

Gemila, the child of the desert, in her tent on the Sahara, whom I had read about at school in *Seven Little Sisters.* ❧

Since Kitty still hung around, and I didn't want to get a scolding, I stayed carefully concealed, waiting for a chance to escape. I finally lay down, my head on my arms.

It was warm, the rug was soft, and before long I fell fast asleep. I was awakened by the sound of voices, high-pitched laughter and people approaching. The dinner party had arrived. I was frozen with horror. They were already moving into the dining room. I sat up breathless, watching while chairs were pulled out, and feet began appearing under the table. I realized I was trapped, and there I would have to stay until the dinner party was over.

I sat back and surveyed the array of feet under the tablecloth. The men's were mostly uniform, black silk socks and neat black pumps. The ladies' were all colors—pink, white, or blue satin slippers to match their dresses. I could reach out and touch any number of them. The conversation flowed easily; women's voices mingling with the deep bass of the men's, much laughter and chatter, the clatter of knives and forks and the ring of glasses. Course after course went by. How could they possibly eat so much? I wondered.

One of the men had slipped his feet out of his pumps, which were apparently too tight for him. He wriggled his toes comfortably under the table. I wondered wickedly what would happen if I leaned forward gently and moved the shoes into another position far away. I also contemplated softly tickling one of the silken insteps near me. They would think there was a mouse under the table, and I imagined the shrieks that would arise and abandoned the idea.

A lady dropped her handkerchief and leaned down to retrieve it. I shrank back as far as possible against the table pillar, holding my breath. What if she saw me under there? I would have to come out, and what would happen to me then? But she didn't see me, and while she was feeling around for it, the hand of the gentleman next to her also appeared in the search. He found it immediately and pressed it into her hand. But instead of letting go, the two hands clasped under the tablecloth and remained locked in that position for about five minutes. I watched this in fascination. I had looked at the place cards, and I knew the lady was Mrs. G; also that the gentleman next to her was not *Mr.* G. Finally the lady withdrew her fingers reluctantly and continued her dinner. This was thrilling. I wondered if they were in love and what Mr. G. thought about it, and if he knew that Mrs. G. was holding hands under the table with Mr. W., a handsome bachelor. ✥

By now, however, I was beginning to tire of my cramped position and wished the long, drawn-out affair would come to an

✥ *Despite the Victorian era's buttoned-down reputation, Mr. W. and Mrs. G. were engaging in fairly common behavior. Though divorce rates were low in the late 1800s, extramarital affairs seem to have been common— particularly in the West, where numerous high-profile scandals (such as the Tabor case) created an image of a freewheeling but socially reprobate society.*

end. But it seemed to go on and on. Finally the last course was eaten, the chairs were pushed back, and the ladies departed, either for the parlor or upstairs to my sister's room "to powder."

Alas, I was not yet freed from confinement. The gentlemen now settled down to smoke, drink, and discuss politics. The chairs, however, were at least pulled out of the way, so I could stretch out and relieve my aching knees. I was tired and hungry and wanted to go to bed. At last, I heard my father asking if they should join the ladies, and the room was deserted.

The maids were apparently all in the kitchen, eating. I crawled stiffly out from under the tablecloth. The door to the pantry swung open, and Mary appeared. She uttered a stifled scream and looked at me in amazement.

"Mother of God, what are you doing under the table? I thought you were in bed long ago. Have you been there all evening? Have you had any dinner?"

I shook my head miserably. I knew if I went out in the kitchen it would cause a commotion among all the maids.

"Whisht now," said Mary, after I had explained the situation, "run up the back stairs and get into bed quickly, and I'll bring up a plate of something to eat."

I slipped through the entryway and scurried up the back stairs to my room. In five minutes I had undressed and was in my night dress. Mary appeared at the door with a tray. I eyed it hungrily. Meat, vegetables, a plate of the rich yellow ice cream and some little confectioner's cakes. Good, kind Mary! For forty years after I had last seen her, even into her bedridden old age, she continued to send a card that reached me every Christmas with the good wishes of that faithful Irish heart.

"Don't tell anyone, will you?" I begged, as she set the tray beside me on the bed.

"Niver a word to anyone. Be a good gurrl now and eat your dinner and go to sleep. It'll be just a secret between us two."

She went out sofly, closing the door behind her. I fell to with relish on the belated dinner.

The Majesty of the Mountains

When spring came along, there was always an annual debate as to whether we could afford a trip east this year or whether we would go up to the mountains for our summer vacation.

Westerners living at such high altitude seemed to feel the need to get down to sea level every so often; or perhaps that was just an excuse for a journey which everyone who could afford it took on the slightest provocation. People traveled back and forth to New York or the West Coast as casually as they set out for Colorado Springs, seventy miles away.

This was a perpetual source of wonder to my father's family, who all lived in New Jersey, commuted to New York, and thought any trip west of Buffalo as hazardous an undertaking as going to Africa.

My father loved the sea and longed for a glimpse of it every so often. Also, he wanted to see his brothers and his sister, for whom, in spite of the distance between them both in miles and temperament, he had a deep and abiding affection. He was particularly fond of his sister, Katherine, who had never married but had gone to keep house for Uncle Jay when his wife died in childbirth.

So every other summer or so, we planned to go east to the seashore. My mother and I generally started a few weeks in advance of my father, and the others joined us when they could. Of course, we always had to stop off in the Oranges to see the relatives, either going or coming.

I am sure my mother disliked these family visits, although she never openly admitted it. She and Aunt Katherine corresponded dutifully several times a year, writing long and gossipy letters about the doings of the various families. Separated by three thousand miles, they got along amicably enough. But face to face in the same house they were far too much alike to be congenial, both being strong-willed and decidedly opinionated.

Aunt Katherine was a tall, aristocratic-looking spinster with fading, yellowish hair, which she wore high on her head in a sort of doughnut, with a frizzed bang over her forehead. Her eyeglasses dangled on a black ribbon around her neck. She was nervous, fidgety, and dictatorial, but for all that she had an alert mind and a keen wit, and when she was not complaining about

The Oranges, a cluster of four New Jersey towns just west of Newark, were a bustling industrial center in the 1890s, with a concentration of hat manufacturers (twenty-one local firms employing 3,700 workers) and a slowly emerging brewery business. Many hotels, stables, restaurants, and other tourist-oriented businesses catered to travelers on the Mount Pleasant Turnpike, which ran right by the Oranges.

one or another of her ailments she could be downright amusing. But having been born before Freudian insights had gained currency, she was forever in the hands of doctors, who prescribed pills and lotions and trips to Richfield Springs, ❦ none of which seemed to do her any good. She was afraid of burglars, fires, thunderstorms, mice, and dogs, and every night she carried the table silver upstairs in a sturdy wicker basket and placed it under her bed.

She had once gone out, in her youthful days, to visit my parents in Central City, and it had been the high spot of her career. But she had failed in her ulterior purpose which, though politely veiled, had been quite evidently to secure a husband. My mother had done her duty and presented her to every eligible bachelor in the neighborhood, but while she was both handsome and witty in her youth, men tended to shy away from her too-bossy manner and her nervous little mannerisms.

She always wore a gold ring with a solitaire pearl on the third finger of her left hand and gave me to understand that it represented some romance in her life, as indeed it must have. But the romance never came to anything. I never learned what broke off the affair with the young man she had set her heart on, but she came back east without him, and the young man, as in the fashion of young men, soon got over it and married someone else, leaving poor Aunt

❦ *The waters of Richfield Springs had the same type of reputation that Colorado's magical air enjoyed among tuberculosis patients. The springs, in upstate New York, became enormously popular after the Civil War. People came from up and down the eastern seaboard, hoping to draw upon the springs' miraculous healing powers. However, most of these curative effects—like Colorado's "altitude cure" for tuberculosis—were purely imaginary.*

108

Katherine to live out her days as an unappreciated and crotchety old maid.

It was a great trial to her that my father had been weaned away from the Episcopal fold in which all the Young family had been reared. Uncle Jay and Uncle Bertram were both vestrymen in the church, and Aunt Katherine, an ardent Episcopalian, was constantly quoting her rector, whom she enshrined on a level just a little below the Deity. All the members of my mother's family were Congregationalists, and she found it hard to understand how my father could worship in such a low church when everyone knew that Congregationalists were almost as unorthodox as Unitarians, who were practically not Christians at all.

Uncle Jay and Aunt Katherine lived in a white frame house built in the 1870s and set far back from the street on a pleasant, tree-shaded lawn.✸ Inside it was strictly mid-Victorian, with a multiplicity of stiff-backed horsehair sofas, rocking chairs, fringed mantel pieces, and clocks in glass houses. It was lit only by gas and kerosene lamps. I thought it horribly dark and gloomy, like Uncle Jay himself, and couldn't wait for the visit to end.

The staircase was a dark little well in the back hall lit only by a skylight. It wound round and round almost perpendicularly like the stairs of a lighthouse, each carpeted tread like a wedge-shaped piece of pie. This staircase aggravated my mother beyond

✸ *The house stood at 61 Glenwood Avenue in East Orange. Jay Young lived there until his death in 1924; Katherine remained there until here own death in 1929.*

words. "Mercy," she would mutter in great annoyance as we crept cautiously down, clinging to the railing, "this stairway is a perfect menace. Someday someone will break their neck on it. I should think Kate would do something about it." But it was not Kate's house, and Uncle Jay was not for any newfangled innovations.

The small square guest room which we occupied had Delft blue wallpaper and a faded blue rug. The bed, a large double mahogany one with a spotless Marseilles spread, took up most of the room, and above it on the wall hung a framed motto: "God Bless Our Home." In the corner there was a chest of drawers, on which stood a daguerreotype of Uncle Jay and his bride taken on their honeymoon, ❦ apparently in a snowstorm, and a huge pincushion with an army of black and white-headed pins arranged neatly to form a pattern. What a pity, I thought, if someone had urgent need of a pin, but I hated to spoil the pattern.

❦ *Daguerreotypes were extremely dangerous and complicated to produce. The image was captured on two highly polished metal plates, which had been treated with chemicals before being placed in the camera. The shutter was opened, and the plates were exposed for about half a minute while the subjects sat very still. The plates were then placed over heated mercury fumes, immersed in hypo-sulfate, then covered with heated gold chloride—certainly nothing to be undertaken by a novice.*

Under the window was a washstand with a blue bowl and pitcher, and a slop jar on the floor beside it. The towels were racked on the side, and the soap dish contained a fresh cake of Pears soap. I eyed the washbowl with distaste. I hated washing in a washbowl, and we had long ago discarded such old-fashioned equipment.

There was, of course, a bathroom at the end of the hall, but Uncle Jay monopolized that in the morning for his bath and shave, so we all had to wait until Aunt Katherine tapped gently on the door and announced that the bathroom was empty. She said "bahth" instead of "bath," as we did.

When we came downstairs Uncle Jay would be eating his breakfast, a fat gold watch open beside his plate. He was a heavily built man with a forbidding nose, deep-set dark eyes, and bushy brows that seemed to be perpetually frowning. After asking us how we had slept and making a few conventional remarks about the weather, he retired behind *The New York Sun* to finish his eggs. This done, he seized his Derby hat and gold-headed cane and, bidding us goodbye, made off for the station to catch the 8:15 for the city. ⚜

⚜ The 8:15 commuter could have been on either the Lackawanna or the Pennsylvania Railroad, both of which had direct service from East Orange to New York City. Neither line, however, had a bridge across the Hudson until after 1900. Commuters debarked on the New Jersey bank and took a ferry across the river into Manhattan.

I always breathed a sigh of relief when Uncle Jay had left the house. He seemed to move in an aura of rectitude and deep gloom. He had a sepulchral voice, and although he tried his best to be jovial with his small niece from the West, it was hard going. His humor was as heavy as his eyebrows. He was still mourning the loss of his wife and, like Queen Victoria, took pleasure in nurturing his grief, though Aunt Helen had been dead more than twenty years.

I distinctly remember one Thanksgiving Day we happened to be at the house and a number of the family had been gathered together for dinner. When the turkey was brought in, instead of picking up the carving knife and fork, as I expected him to do, after grace had been said, he reached for the glass of port before him and rose to his feet.

"Before we begin," he announced in a voice choked with emotion, "let us drink to the memory of those dear ones who have left us but are still with us in spirit."

With this he sat down and, taking out his handkerchief, openly wiped his eyes.

There was a ghastly silence. Everyone took a hasty sip of wine. I was overcome with embarrassment and stared at my plate, hoping with all my heart that he would not start to cry. Aunt Katherine, biting her lips, saved the day by picking up the little bell beside her plate and asking the maid to pass the cranberry sauce. The conversation gradually came to life again, but such a damper had been put on the entire proceedings that the dinner never regained what one would call a sprightly mood.

When Uncle Jay was safely on his way to New York, the house seemed to draw a deep breath and relax. Aunt Katherine would order a surrey from the livery stable, since they kept no horses, and we would jog comfortably over to Uncle Bertram's house, four blocks away.

Uncle Bertram was the youngest of the three brothers, rather stout and balding and far more genial than Uncle Jay. In his later years he even unbent enough to play golf, whacking the ball about the course with great earnestness and concentration. He, too, was a widower, and had had to call on

The Young family claimed descent from some fairly illustrious figures. The purported founder of the lineage in North America, Thomas Mayhew, came to the New World in

an unmarried sister to keep house for him and bring up his daughter, a quiet, serious-minded girl, slightly older than I.

I would far have preferred staying at Uncle Bertram's house, for Aunt Mollie was a lively, talkative person, and the atmosphere was quite different from the somber rigidity of Uncle Jay's. But Aunt Katherine always let it be understood that Uncle Jay was the Head of the Family, and it was proper for us to stay there, especially since Aunt Mollie was only a half-sister, a member of my grandfather's second family.

There were nine or ten of these half-uncles and aunts, most of whom I never met or ever knew by name. The two families rarely mingled, and the only ones I was familiar with were Aunt Mollie and Aunt Grace, a meek, unobtrusive person who later came to keep house and act as a companion for Aunt Katherine. She took the latter's domination without a murmur, but Aunt Mollie was a peppery person and occasionally stood up to her half-sister, and then such violent arguments would rage that people thought it just as well when Uncle Bertram, who worked for the Lackawanna Railroad, was moved to Scranton, and Aunt Katherine had the field to herself.

For all her peculiarities, I was genuinely fond of Aunt Katherine, for underneath her outer shell of fussiness and inhibitions beat the kindest of hearts, and she was a

1631; he was a colonial governor in Massachusetts and co-founder of Nantucket and Martha's Vineyard. Another forefather, William Swift, also reached America in 1631 and founded the Massachusetts town of Sandwich. Several generations down the line, an ancestor named Isaac Swift served as George Washington's staff surgeon at Valley Forge.

deeply devoted and loyal sister to her three brothers. Nevertheless, I was glad when the visit came to an end, and we could proceed up the coast to Massachusetts.

I enjoyed the sea, but my true heart lay back in the mountains, where every other year we vacationed at a lakeside hotel. On their part, the Rogers family almost invariably went camping. As they prepared to go, I would be over at their house watching them get ready, assembling their paraphernalia, beds, tents, blankets, canned goods, etc. How I envied them! They were going straight up into the wildest part of the mountains, and there, by the side of some clear, sparkling trout stream, they would settle down to fish, hunt, eat over a campfire, and enjoy the thrills of a pioneer life. ❧

They set off at 7 in the morning, dressed in their heavy mountain clothing, the girls in wool blouses and divided skirts, with long laced boots up to their knees and wide felt hats. They all piled into the heavy wagon loaded to the breaking point, the frying pans rattling and the tent poles sticking out behind. The doctor picked up the reins, clicked to the horses, and started the cavalcade slowly westward down Colfax Avenue, at the end of which, fifteen miles away, the peaks of the Rockies glittered in the bright morning sun.

I sadly turned back into my own house. Why hadn't I been born into a large, hearty family like that instead of being practically

❧ *The Rogers children would remain devoted wilderness lovers throughout their lives. The eldest, James (see page 24), went on to found the Colorado Mountain Club in 1912, while Edmund had a long career with the National Park Service—first as superintendent of Rocky Mountain National Park, then in the same post at Yellowstone. Upon his retirement in 1961, Edmund received the Distinguished Service Award for his many Park Service achievements.*

an only child? But by the following week my father might announce that instead of going east this summer we would all go up to Wellington Lake for a month. I jumped up and down with glee. The Rogers might go camping, which was more romantic, but no one in his senses could say that life in the mountains anywhere at that time was not primitive, even if we didn't actually sleep in tents.

We started at 8 in the morning, taking the little, rickety narrow-gauge railroad that clattered along twenty miles or so, paralleling the mountains until it reached the mouth of Platte Canyon, where the South Platte River dashed out of the gorge to the freedom of the plains below.※ Here the train turned westward, twisting and turning up the canyon, following the bends in the creek. Here we were between bare, brown foothills studded with jutting rocks. The train, with its red plush seats, smelled horribly of cinders, smoke, popcorn, and bananas. It creaked and whined around curves while we battled with hermetically sealed windows for a breath of air and tried to keep down our breakfasts.

After two hours we had gone thirty miles and arrived at Buffalo Park. We climbed out of the train, queasy and considerably shaken, drawing in great breaths of the fresh pine-scented air. A leathery ranchman was waiting at the station with a buckboard and a team of white horses.

※ The railroad, built in the 1870s as the Denver, South Park and Pacific, had by the 1890s been absorbed by the Colorado and Southern, a competitor of the mighty Denver & Rio Grande Western. The route ascended what today is known as Waterton Canyon, following the present-day Colorado Trail along the North Fork of the South Platte River, and continued west over Kenosha Pass into South Park and points west.

Rattling over the log bridge across the creek, we headed into the mountains. It was a twelve-mile drive to the lake, practically all upgrade; the last hill was nine miles long.

As we wound further and further up, the bare foothills were left behind, and the mountain became a dark and living green with the density of pine interspersed with the delicate trembling white of the quaking aspen. Chipmunks darted here and there, flirting their tails impudently. The woods were thick with columbine, Indian paintbrush, and red kinnikinnick berries.

The horses strained and staggered with the load. Mr. Dickinson, the driver, reined them in as we rounded the curb. "Fine view," he said tersely, pointing with his whip. It was perhaps the first word he had uttered during the entire trip. We all climbed out to look about while the horses rested.

For miles a vast panorama of wooded peaks stretched as far as the eye could see. Far, far below us the creek boiled and fumed over its stony bed. A hawk wheeled and dipped in the sky, but there was no sound in all those miles of wilderness except the tired breathing of the horses and the sound of a pebble dropping onto the rocks below. It was a fine view indeed.

Before long the road widened into a clearing, and we could glimpse the sight of water among the trees. This was the summer resort of Wellington Lake. It boasted a hotel and two cottages. The hotel was a

*Wellington Lake was named for James Wellington Nesmith, yet another of the Youngs' old Central City associates. Nesmith, a machinist and railroad builder, helped construct

small, red frame structure with a sagging front porch. There was also a barn and a shed, and two outhouses standing chastely side by side farther up the mountain.

Inside the hotel the sitting room had a linoleum floor, a stove, three wooden chairs, and a table. There were three bedrooms upstairs and two down, each with a double bed, a rickety bureau, and a washstand. We hung our clothes on the hooks along the wall and raced down to the shore of the lake. It was about five miles around and lay encircled by darkly forested mountians except at one end, where there towered a huge pile of red sandstone rocks known as Giant's Castle.

In the early morning the lake lay clear and transclucent, mirroring the trees and the rocks. Not a ripple stirred the stillness except for the occasional leap of a fish. That was my father's favorite time for fishing, or perhaps in the late afternoon when the mountains cast long shadows and the sun went down in fiery splendor behind the massive boulders of Giants Castle. Then the lake water turned to molten silver.

We would climb into one of the heavy, flat-bottomed row boats and row quietly out into the middle of the lake. All one had to do was to cast a line lightly into the water, and in less than no time a trout would be struggling on the hook. Putting them into a little wicker basket, we would come home triumphantly with a nice catch to be fried

the Colorado Central into Gilpin County and was among the many benefactors of the Central City Opera House. Nesmith later moved to Denver and became president of Colorado Iron Works; he lived about fifteen blocks east of the Youngs, at 1100 East Colfax Avenue. A number of other Young family associates held ownership stakes in the Wellington Lake property. Two, Charles Cobb and Harper Orahood, served alongside Frank Young on the Fairmount Cemetery board of directors; a third, W.S. Morse, was William Bush's business partner.

for breakfast in the morning. There is nothing sweeter than the taste of a freshly caught rainbow trout. Fishing in the creeks was sportier and meant far more casting, but my father was satisfied merely to sit in a boat and trail a line behind.

Sometimes we would go ashore on the far side of the lake and walk through the green mountain meadows studded with yellow tiger lilies and tall brown cattails. There were quantities of wild berries here, too, to be gathered and made into jelly, and it was fun to scratch the big globules of spruce gum that hung on the trees and chew it. It crackled at first, but once chewed up it had a clean aromatic taste and made very satisfactory gum—just as good, I thought, as the Beeman's Pepsin or White's Yucatan that we bought in the stores.

There were always saddle horses to be had, and we would often follow the sandy trail around the lake. An occasional coyote would run slinking through the trees, and once a bobcat dropped off a limb just in front of us, frightening the horses.

The Youngs probably rented their horses from the Wellington Hotel, the more elaborate of the lake's two hotels. The family stayed at the much more modest Higginson homestead, built in about 1877. The Wellington, which opened some time during the 1890s, boasted thirty guest rooms. Ten furnished guest cottages also dotted the shore, and the Silver Spruce Guest Ranch stood a few miles down the road.

Sometimes we drove or rode up to Runner's Ranch, eight miles away, for meat. This was a lonely, hardly discernible trail through the woods, and the ranch stood far away, high on top of one of the ranges. There was a family of children, wild looking, like little woods colts, so unused to seeing people that they would scatter away and hide when the wagon came in sight. I pitied them, so far away on this lonely mountain. However, they didn't live there in winter but moved down to the metropolitan center of Buffalo Park, where there was a one-room school, a store, and a post office. ❧

Every day we fished, we walked, we drove, and we climbed mountains. Unfortunately the icy lake water, with its shelving banks and unplumbed depths, did not permit swimming. We enjoyed it all to the hilt, and by the time three weeks or more had passed, I had ceased to envy the Rogers on their camping trip.

The short mountain summer was passing. Wild geese honked over the lake. The sky grew even more clear and blue, and the sun shone with almost a hint of sadness in it. Soon the snow would begin to fall, a chill wind would sweep across the lake, and the little settlement would be boarded up and ice bound for nine long months in the heavy mountain snows. It would be nice to get back to civilization again, to bathe in a real tub instead of a washtub heated in the blacksmith's shack over a wood fire, to eat something besides beans, boiled potatoes, soda biscuits, and corned beef.

I had been glad to come, but I was also glad when the buckboard appeared at the door again to take us away. We were tanned, bursting with health, and we had a lovely basket of fish to take home with us. There was no straining now on the part of the horses. The trouble was to hold back on the

❧ *Buffalo Park (a.k.a. Buffalo Creek) was an important logging center during the 1880s, supplying building materials to fast-growing Denver and railroad ties to Colorado's ever-expanding rail network. Tourist traffic from Denver increased manyfold in the late 1890s, when Colorado Fuel & Iron executive John Jerome built a summer home in the area. Jerome spent a couple of years as the school principal at Central City in the early 1870s; one of his teachers there was Carrie Sims Young.*

hill. The brakes screeched and groaned, as the wagon wheels locked, swayed, and swerved perilously near the edge of the road, with its sheer drop to the bottom of the canyon far below. Once down the hill we trotted briskly into Buffalo Park just in time. The four-coach train was already panting gently in the station. With one last gulp of fresh mountain air, we climbed into the stuffy, cindery coach. "Alllll Abooooard!" shouted the conductor. The train shuddered, gathered momentum, and swung sickeningly around the curve. We were on our way. Summer was over.

By contrast, the train that bore us home after our journeys to the East was an elaborate affair, and traveling in the relative luxury it offered created one of the high spots of a trip East. I loved those trains and, on the return trip, would willingly have continued straight on through to the Pacific Coast.

If I could persuade my mother to do so, we would push our way the whole length of the long train, struggling with the heavy doors, and ensconce ourselves on two camp chairs on the back platform. This platform was open to the elements, and the wind whipped cindery dust into the eyes and clothing of those who chose to sit there; but a few intrepid souls would occasionally join us to watch the long shining stretch of rails disappearing behind us over the prairies, as far as the eye could see.

At night, curled up in the berth beside my mother (who never removed any of her clothing except her dress and shoes, in order to be ready for an emergency), I would cautiously raise the curtain and lie for hours peering out of the window.

As we rattled through some small town in the Midwest, with its dimly lit, deserted streets, I wondered about the people living in all those little houses. Overhead the sky was a blue vault, splintered with millions of stars. I loved the clackety-clack of the wheels as we rushed steadily westward, and the wild plaintive shriek of the locomotive as it left a town and plunged into the vast black country ahead, like the cry of a lost soul.

But best of all was waking up in the early morning when the train was climbing the great high open plains. In the clear, ruddy light you could see for miles—nothing in sight but the small, red frame station; perhaps a lonely red ranch house in the distance, with its inevitable windmill.

Eventually distant nubbins would appear on the horizon to the west, and before long the entire expanse of the Colorado Rockies would sweep up from the plains in a magnificent crescendo of white-clad peaks. Never have I seen this sight without a catch in my throat, without a burst of joy in my heart, knowing that I am a child of that place, nurtured by the spirit and splendor of those majestic mountains.

Epilogue

*I*N KEEPING WITH FAMILY TRADITION, Elizabeth Young became a fine musician—a singer, like her mother and her Aunt Hattie. After graduating from the Wolcott School in 1909, she studied voice with Hattie and became a well-regarded amatuer soloist, performing at churches, in local opera productions, and eventually on stages as prominent as the Broadway Theater and Elitch's Gardens. Elizabeth gained enough renown to rate periodic reviews in the Denver newspapers. In a typical notice, for an August 1913 concert at Elitch's, the *Denver Post* praised Elizabeth's "fresh young voice, gracious personality, and decided technical understanding." Her appreciative audience that evening brought her out for an encore, "I Hear a Thrush at Eve"—which, the *Post* raved, was "deliciously presented by Miss Young."

Elizabeth also spent two years at Bennett College in upstate New York, where she roomed with a daughter of the distinguished Muhlenberg family of Pennsylvania. One Muhlenberg ancestor, Henry Melchior Muhlenberg, had established the North American branch of the Lutheran Church in the mid-eighteenth century. Another, Frederick A. Muhlenberg, was the first Speaker of the U.S. House of Representatives; his signature is on the Bill of Rights. A third forefather, Peter Muhlenberg, was one of George Washington's brigadier generals during the Revolutionary War—in which, coincidentally, he served alongside army field surgeon Isaac Swift, one of Frank Young's ancestors.

The two families renewed their old association permanently in 1917, when Elizabeth became engaged to her roommate's brother, Frederick Muhlenberg, a lieutenant in the U.S. Army. The two set their wedding day for November 11, 1917. But a few days before the nuptials, Muhlenberg's unit (the 314th Infantry) received orders to ship out for Europe and World War I. Rather than postpone their union indefinitely, Frederick and Elizabeth exchanged their vows on November 10, then bid adieu until after the war. Elizabeth spent those long months in Annapolis, Maryland. Lieutenant Muhlenberg did his lineage proud, returning with a Purple Heart, a Distinguished Service Cross, a Croix de Guerre, and a Legion d'Honore.

After the war, the Muhlenbergs settled in Frederick's hometown of Reading, Pennsylvania. An architect by training, he opened his own firm, which prospered in the fat postwar years. Frederick designed a number of notable buildings in downtown Reading and made enough of a name for himself to win election to the city council. Elizabeth, meanwhile, quickly rose to social prominence, not only for her singing voice (which she displayed frequently in informal performances) but also as the founder of the local Junior League chapter. She gave birth to a daughter, Betty, in 1920, and three more children followed: Caroline in 1923, Frederica in 1926, and John David in 1929.

The Muhlenberg household was as cultured and civic-minded as the Young household at 244 West Colfax had been. The latter address, however, no longer existed, and the residents had scattered. Elizabeth's father died in 1919, the year before his first grandchild was born; the Denver Post eulogized him as "a man of quiet ways, of courteous manners, tinged with the dignity and simplicity of 'the old school.'" He was buried in Fairmount Cemetery, alongside many other Colorado pioneers. Carrie, Eleanor, and Hattie continued to live at 244 West Colfax until 1924, when the house was razed to make way for the new Denver City and County Building. Hattie Sims moved into to an apartment on Capitol Hill, two blocks from her studio. Carrie and Eleanor moved back east and divided their time among relatives in New York, New Jersey, Massachusetts, and Pennsylvania.

They spent their share of time with the Muhlenbergs in Reading, helping Elizabeth cope with the one difficulty she faced at that stage in her life: Her eldest child, Betty, developed cerebral palsy in early childhood. The disease took nothing away from Betty's intellect—she matured into a playful, intelligent individual—but it confined her permanently to a wheelchair; she never took a step. Betty required constant physical care, which her mother provided steadfastly—and without benefit of the specialized technology that today helps patients and caregivers cope with physical challenges. The work could be draining and occasionally drove Elizabeth into periods of exhaustion or depression. But she remained devoted to Betty, performing her special duty with grace for thirty-three years, until her daughter died of breast cancer in 1953.

By then, the Muhlenbergs had confronted many other challenges. In the late 1920s, against his better judgment, Frederick bought an ownership stake in an office building he had designed. The Great Depression undercut the investment and left the family heavily saddled with debt. Reading's building boom ceased, and Frederick's business fell off; for the first time in her forty-plus years, Elizabeth knew material want. Like so many middle-class families of that era, the Muhlenbergs barely managed to make ends meet. They eventually lost their home, but Frederick refused to file for bankruptcy. Though it took nearly thirty years, he ultimately paid back every dime he owed.

The Depression was hard on Elizabeth's mother and sister as well. The Young family estate dwindled to nothing, leaving Carrie and Eleanor nearly bereft of resources. In 1934, with Carrie in failing health, the two returned to Denver and rented an apartment in northwest Denver. After Carrie Young died in 1935, Eleanor left Denver for good. She opened a gift shop in

Maine, which she stocked in part with the Youngs' family possessions, and continued to circulate among friends and family, dividing her time between Massachusetts and New Jersey. Eventually she moved in with Elizabeth and Frederick. She was under their roof when she died on October 1, 1941, aged sixty-seven years.

The Muhlenbergs by that time were living in Alexandria, Virginia. Frederick had returned to the military in 1940, taking a job in the Army Corps of Engineers. After Eleanor's passing, the family moved to Cincinnati, and then to Fort Thomas, Kentucky—wherever Lt. Muhlenberg's assignments took him. The constant uprooting made an outsider of Elizabeth, the first time she had ever known isolation. Her active social life had always been a welcome respite from the demands of caring for Betty; with that outlet closed, Elizabeth's spirits suffered. These were difficult years.

But better ones came after World War II. With the children grown and the economy booming again, the Muhlenbergs moved back to Reading—but they only stayed long enough for Frederick to get himself elected to Congress. The one-time city councilman, a moderate Republican, carried a Pennsylvania district dominated by left-leaning union voters—the very "socialists" Elizabeth had deemed so fearsome as a child on Colfax Avenue. They moved to Washington, and Elizabeth—now fifty-six years of age—had a ball. After so many years of displacement, she found herself back in her element, ensconced in the nation's liveliest social scene. She went to parties, sat on committees, even wrote a weekly column for the *Reading Eagle.*

Her husband, meanwhile, experienced the thrill of serving in the same body his forefeather once ran. The latter-day Frederick Muhlenberg, however, never made it to Speaker of the House. In 1947 he voted for the Taft-Hartley Act, which his labor-minded Reading constituents overwhelmingly opposed. They never forgave him for that vote and rejected his bid for re-election in 1948.

Back in Reading, Frederick revived his long-dormant career as an architect, while Elizabeth—like her father before her—took up the pen and began to write. She had started a novel back in the 1930s, a romance in the Gone With the Wind vein; after Betty's death, Elizabeth finally had the time to complete the project. Though never published, it provided an outlet for the artistic spirit that so infused all the Youngs. She wrote *On Colfax Avenue* in the 1960s, in the last years of her life.

Elizabeth died on October 1, 1967, eight days shy of her seventy-seventh birthday—and about a century after her parents first traveled west to Colorado. Her own journey had brought her back east, to a world somewhat older and wearier than the one in which she'd grown up. But not all that different, perhaps; for she still managed to experience the adventure, the sense of joyous self-discovery, that are every Coloradan's birthright.